READER'S DIGEST

Festival of Popular Songs

Editor: William L. Simon
Associates: Mary Kelleher, Elizabeth Mead   Copy Editor: Natalie Moreda
Art: Nicholas Calabrese, Dana Burns

Music arranged and edited by Dan Fox

Introductions to songs by John S. Wilson

The Reader's Digest Association, Inc.
Pleasantville, New York   Montreal

Library of Congress Catalog Card Number 77-24818

ISBN 0-89577-035-0

Printed in the United States of America

Third Printing, October 1981

index to sections

index to songs

introduction

Ask a Brahms lover to name his or her favorite of the composer's four symphonies, and invariably the answer is, "The last one I heard."

This is our fourth Reader's Digest Songbook, and at this time we'd have to say it's our favorite—until we replay one of the others!

All Reader's Digest songbooks are designed to provide instant pleasure to performers with a wide range of tastes and even to those with quite limited skills. The brand-new arrangements by Dan Fox, specially commissioned for these books, are easy to play, but at the same time they make the player sound stylishly modern and professional.

There are several features unique to this book. Foremost, of course, is the repertoire, which does not duplicate any selections in our previous books. About 25 percent of our collection is music that has become popular (very popular!) during the last 15 years. In selecting these contemporary hits, we imposed our usual high standards: they had to be playable, singable, durable, and enjoyable—to any and all performers. "Here today, gone tomorrow" record hits—songs that come to life only through electronic indulgence or songs that can be performed effectively *only* by the originating artists —did not qualify.

For the first time, at the request of many of our songbook owners, we have included some instrumental selections, mainly for pianists and organists. They may require a little more practice than some of the pop tunes, but you'll find our arrangements much easier than the originals and well worth any extra effort. We also feature a small but select children's section, with songs that should be equally appealing to adults, and it's up-to-date enough to include two *Sesame Street* "classics" along with that "most popular reindeer [song] of all"—Rudolph, of red-nosed fame.

A few words on how to use the book

On all but the strictly instrumental selections, we have vocal lines with a piano or organ accompaniment. The melody line (with stems turned up unless it stands alone) may also be played by any solo treble-clef C-instrument, including violin, flute, recorder, oboe, and harmonica.

The small notes in the bass line (with stems turned down) are pedal notes for the organ. These have been kept within an octave range so that they may be used with most standard models. They are not applicable to small, simple chord organs.

For guitarists, the diagrams above the staves indicate by the simplest method known where to put your fingers on the fret board. Of course, those guitarists who prefer to invent their own voicings may follow the chord symbols.

These same chord symbols can be the guide to pianists who have studied the popular chord method; they can read the melody line and improvise their own left-hand accompaniments. And they can provide a part for bass players, both string and brass; just play the root note of each chord symbol, except where another note is indicated (for example "G/D bass"). Accordionists also can use the chord symbols for the buttons played with the left hand. With the right hand on the keyboard, they can play the treble portion of each arrangement as written.

So, you see, with this book you can have an instrumental ensemble, a solo recital with or without accompaniment, or a grand old sing-along session. For the latter, we've also provided a separate booklet, *Sing Along!*, that includes all the lyrics to all the songs in this *Festival of Popular Songs*.

Now, we hope that you'll enjoy your songbook as much as we've enjoyed preparing it for you!

—The Editors

Somewhere, My Love

Words by Paul Francis Webster   Music by Maurice Jarre

"Lara's Theme" kept welling up throughout the film Doctor Zhivago. It was the musical accompaniment for the character, played by Julie Christie, who was the great love of Zhivago's life in the adaptation of Boris Pasternak's 1958 Nobel Prize-winning novel. The Russian Pasternak rejected the prize for political reasons, but the prize-winning aura of his work continued into the film re-creation when Maurice Jarre's score won the composer his second Academy Award in 1965. (His first was for his score for Lawrence of Arabia in 1962.) "Lara's Theme" emerged as a hit song in 1966, when Paul Francis Webster adapted it and added the lyrics that turned it into "Somewhere, My Love."

(Lara's Theme from the Metro-Goldwyn-Mayer Motion Picture Doctor Zhivago)

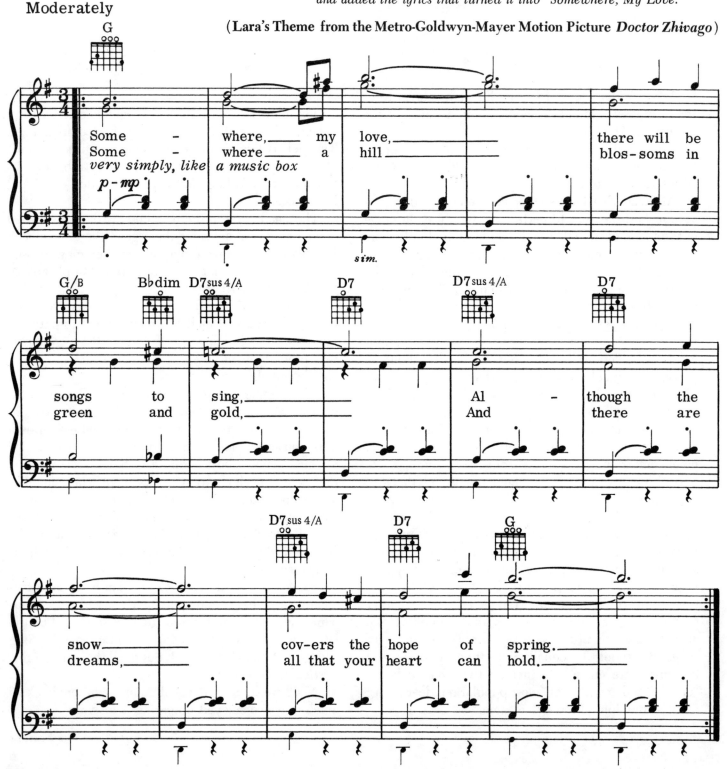

Till then,_____ my sweet,_____ think of me
(Lar - a,_____ my own,)

p music box again

now and then._____ God - speed, my

love,_____ till you are mine_____

a - gain._____

pp
(like a ghostly echo)

8va--------

8va bassa----

7

The Shadow of Your Smile

(Love Theme from the Metro-Goldwyn-Mayer Motion Picture *The Sandpiper*)

Words by Paul Francis Webster   Music by Johnny Mandel

Moderately, with a Latin feeling

No chord / The shad-ow of your smile when you are gone ___ Will col-or all my dreams and light the

In the history of popular song, few writers have approached the quantity and quality of lyricist Johnny Mercer. In 1961 and 1962 he won both a film Academy Oscar and a recording Academy Grammy for "Moon River" and "Days of Wine and Roses," respectively. Naturally, he was first choice when the producer of The Sandpiper commissioned a lyric for an especially appealing theme that Johnny Mandel had composed for the score of the movie. Mercer, though preoccupied at the time with several other projects, gave it a try with a lyric that sought to identify with the film's story, its setting at picturesque Big Sur, its stars Elizabeth Taylor and Richard Burton, and its rather shallow symbolism—a sandpiper with a broken wing, nursed back to health and freedom. When the producer shared Mercer's own lack of enthusiasm for the results, Johnny suggested, "Why don't you get Paul Francis Webster?" Webster ignored the story and the sandpiper and wrote a lyric that simply fitted the mood of the melody. The song, sung by a chorus, accompanied the final credits in the film, and in 1965 it won both an Oscar and a Grammy.

10

Whatever Will Be, Will Be (Que Será, Será)

from *The Man Who Knew Too Much*

In Alfred Hitchcock's 1956 film The Man Who Knew Too Much, *Doris Day played a former Broadway singing star whose small son is kidnaped and held prisoner in a foreign embassy. She visits the embassy and, to attract her son's attention, sings the lullaby she always sang to him. A traditional, familiar lullaby could have been used under the circumstances, but Hitchcock felt it would be much more effective to have a song that could be specifically identified with the mother and child. So he asked Ray Evans and Jay Livingston to write a song that would sound as though it had been handed down through generations. "Whatever Will Be, Will Be," the "folksong" they created, won an Oscar in 1956.*

Words and music by Jay Livingston and Ray Evans

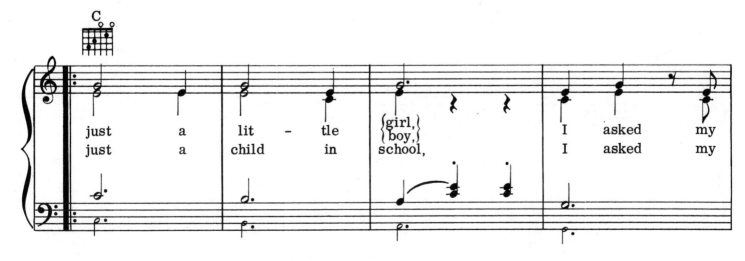

C#dim   Dm7   G7

moth - er,   "What will I be?_____
teach - er,   "What should I try?_____

Dm7   G7

Will   I   be   {pret - ty?}   Will   I   be   rich?"
Should I paint   {hand - some?}   Should I sing   songs?"
    pic - tures?

Dm7   G7   C   (No chord)

Here's what she said to me:_____   "Que se-
This was her wise re - ply:_____

F   C

ra, se - ra,_____   What - ev - er will be, will

12

be; ____ The fu-ture's not ours to see. ____ Que se-

ra, se- ra! ____ What will be, will

be!" ____ When I was ____ Que se-

ra, se- ra!"

The Way We Were

from *The Way We Were*

Marvin Hamlisch—at age 29 and still relatively unknown—won three Oscars in one night. "The Way We Were," the title song of the nostalgic film, was voted the best original song at the Academy Awards ceremony in 1974, and Hamlisch's score for the film was voted the best original dramatic score. In addition, Hamlisch won another Oscar for his scoring and adaptation of Scott Joplin's music, used on the soundtrack of The Sting. For lyricists Alan and Marilyn Bergman the Oscar for "The Way We Were" was their second; they won their first in 1968 for "The Windmills of Your Mind," with music by Michel Legrand.

Words by Alan and Marilyn Bergman
Music by Marvin Hamlisch

Slowly

mp simply

Mem - 'ries   light the cor-ners of my   mind,

Mist-y wa-ter-col-or mem - 'ries_____ of the way we

were.   Scat-tered pic - tures

(mp)

of the smiles we left be - hind,

Smiles we gave to one an-

oth - er _____

for the way we were.

Can it be that it was all so

sim-ple then,

or has time re - writ - ten ev - 'ry

line?

Around the World

from *Around the World in Eighty Days*

When Orson Welles undertook to turn Jules Verne's novel Around the World in Eighty Days into a spectacular Broadway musical in 1946, he created a complicated fiasco involving an aerial ballet; an entire Japanese circus; 40 tons of sets, costumes, and props; and a Cole Porter score that was one of the composer's least distinguished. Surprisingly, for Welles, Porter, and the novel, the disaster proved a prelude to success. Welles went on to one of his greatest roles in the film The Third Man, and Porter's next Broadway musical, Kiss Me, Kate, became a high point of his career. Then, in 1956, Around the World in Eighty Days was turned into a successful musical film for which Victor Young wrote the kind of score, including this haunting title song, that had eluded Cole Porter. Ironically, Michael Todd, the flamboyant showman who produced the movie, was the original producer of Welles' Broadway version but lost interest and turned the production over to Welles.

Words by Harold Adamson   Music by Victor Young

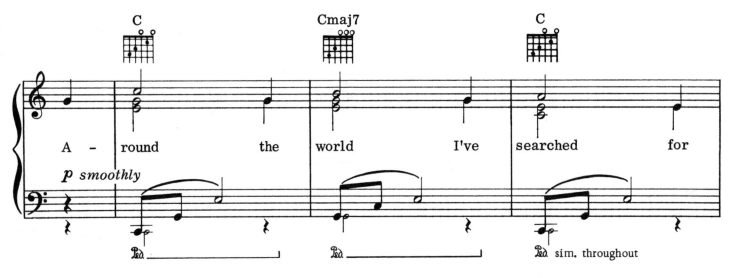

ren - dez - vous. I knew some - where, some-

time, some - how, You'd look at me, and I would

see the smile you're smil - ing now. It

might have been in Coun - ty

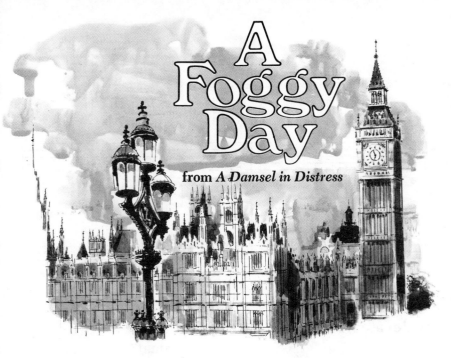

A Foggy Day

from *A Damsel in Distress*

Early in 1937 George and Ira Gershwin were working on what proved to be George's last complete film score (he died in July of that year), A Damsel in Distress, starring Fred Astaire and Joan Fontaine. One night George returned from a party shortly after midnight, took off his dinner jacket, sat down at the piano, and asked Ira if he had any ideas. Ira said that there was a spot in the film where they might do a song about fog. "A Foggy Day in London,'" Ira suggested, "or maybe 'A Foggy Day in London Town.'" George said he preferred the title with "town" in it and immediately started developing a melody. But despite George's preference, the publisher used a shorter title, and the song became "A Foggy Day."

Words by Ira Gershwin
Music by George Gershwin

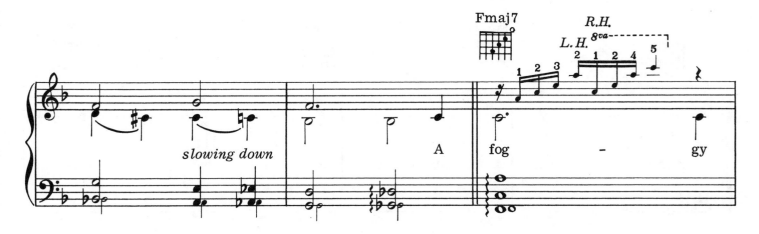

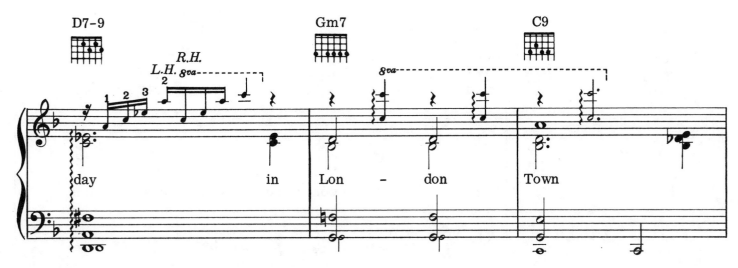

In tempo with a moderate swing

Had me low and had me down. I viewed the morn-ing with a-larm; The Brit-ish Mu-se-um had lost its charm. How long, I won-dered, could this thing

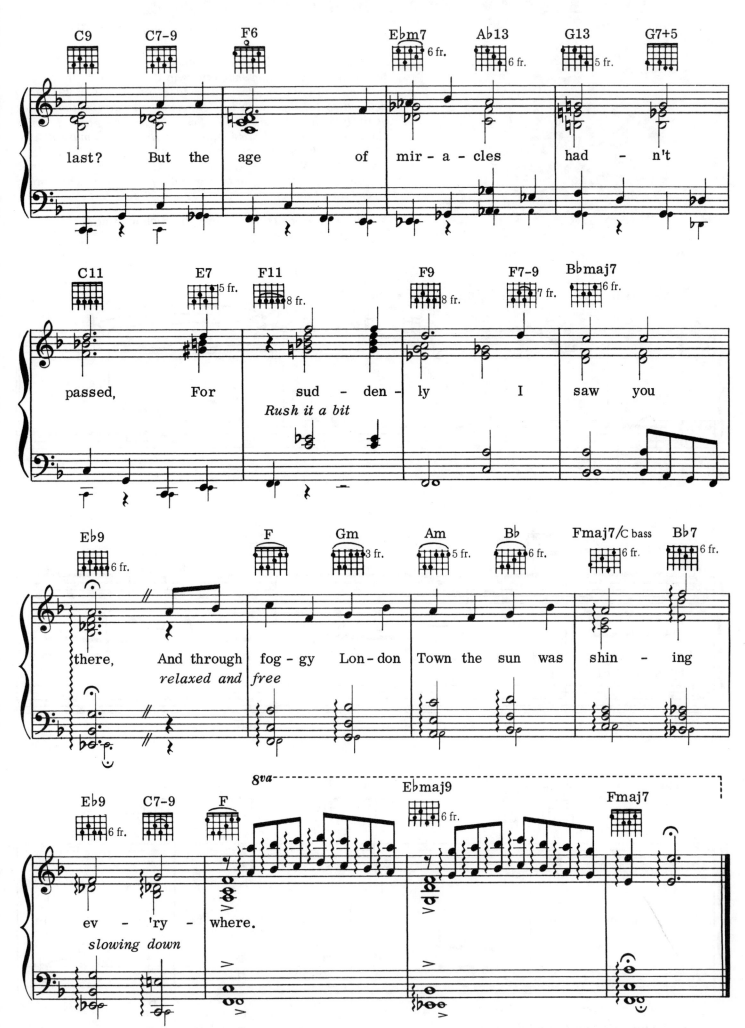

It's Easy To Remember

from the Paramount picture *Mississippi*

*Between 1925 and 1931 Richard Rodgers and Lorenz Hart were two of the most prolific songwriters in the Broadway theater. In 1926 alone they wrote five hit-studded shows. But in 1931 they decided to try their luck in Hollywood, and during their three years there they worked on only five films. And only two of them—*Love Me Tonight *and* Mississippi—*gave them much musical satisfaction. "It's Easy To Remember" was one of three worthy Rodgers and Hart songs that Bing Crosby sang in the 1935 film* Mississippi, *but the songs were largely overlooked by the critics, who instead concentrated their praise on W. C. Fields, Bing's costar.*

Words by Lorenz Hart   **Music by Richard Rodgers**

* *Roll right fist on the white keys.*

24

tight;_____ I'd rath-er dream_____ than have that lone - ly feel - ing

steal - ing through the night._____ Each lit-tle mo - ment_____ Is clear be-

as before

fore me,_____ And though it brings me re - gret; It's eas - y to re-

mem - ber, But so hard to for - get.

slower

Speak Softly Love

(Love Theme from the Paramount picture *The Godfather*)

During the 1950's and 1960's Italian composers suddenly surged to the forefront in writing scores for films. Spearheading this movement were Riz Ortolani, who wrote "More," the theme of Mondo Cane, *and Nino Rota, composer of the score for* La Dolce Vita. *So in 1971, when Francis Ford Coppola wanted music that reflected old-country Italian traditions for the wedding scenes in his production of* The Godfather, *it was only natural that he should turn to Nino Rota, who contributed this love theme, a haunting counterpoint to the violence that colored most of the story about the rise of an American gangster.*

Words by Larry Kusik   Music by Nino Rota

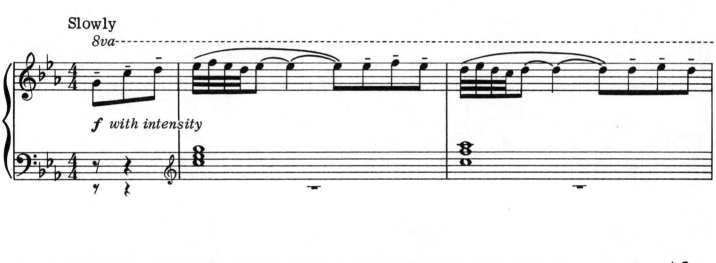

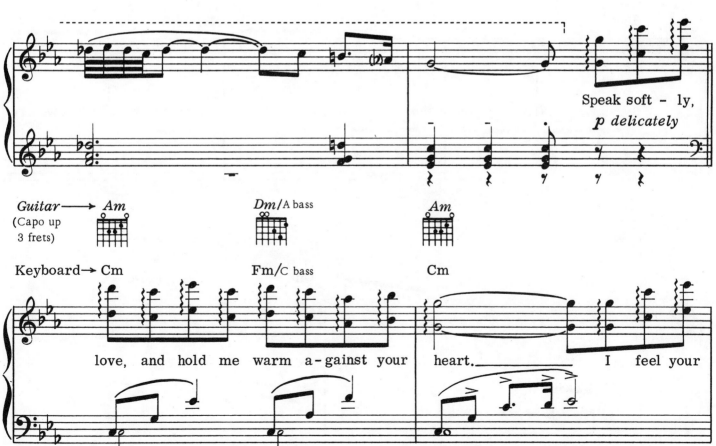

The Way You Look Tonight

Reading or singing the lyrics that Dorothy Fields wrote for Jerome Kern's lovely, lilting melody "The Way You Look Tonight," one would never guess that they are ironic. "Oh, but you're lovely," Fred Astaire sang to Ginger Rogers in Swing Time. "Never, never change . . . keep that breathless charm . . . just the way you look tonight." The way Ginger looked at the moment was awful—or, at least, Hollywood's version of awful: She was in the midst of shampooing her hair. Out of the film, this song (which won an Academy Award in 1936) has always been treated as a charming love song—which, of course, it is. But it just shows how deceptive words, particularly endearing words, can be when they are taken out of context.

from *Swing Time*

Words by Dorothy Fields   Music by Jerome Kern

33

Long Ago
(And Far Away)

from *Cover Girl*

When Gene Kelly sang "Long Ago (And Far Away)" to Rita Hayworth in the 1944 film Cover Girl, no one could have imagined the difficulties that Ira Gershwin had had in trying to find the right lyrics for Jerome Kern's melody. He made more than 40 false starts and completed six different versions. Finally, the film's producer, Arthur Schwartz, a successful songwriter himself, telephoned Gershwin to say that the lyrics had to be finished within two days. Reluctantly, Ira read his latest effort to Schwartz, who took it down and added it to the score. Even then Gershwin felt that "Long Ago" was just "a collection of words adding up to very little." In reality, it added up to a lot: "Long Ago (And Far Away)" sold more copies of sheet music than any other song Ira wrote, including all the hits he created with his brother, George.

Words by Ira Gershwin   Music by Jerome Kern

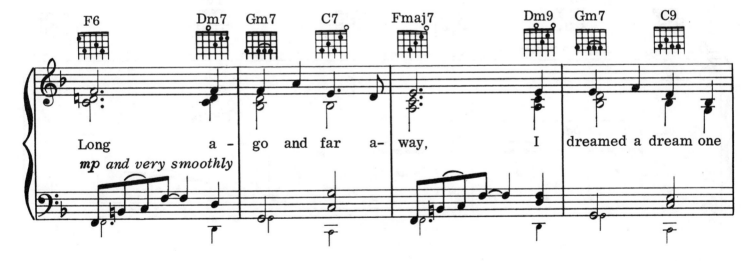

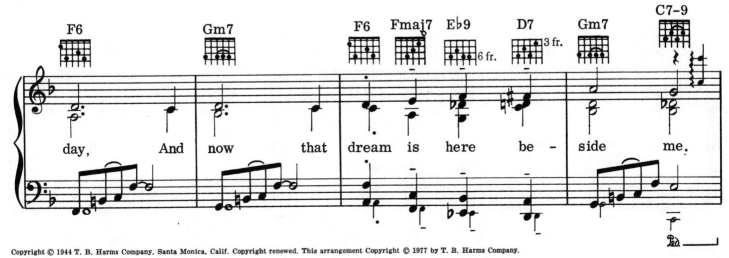

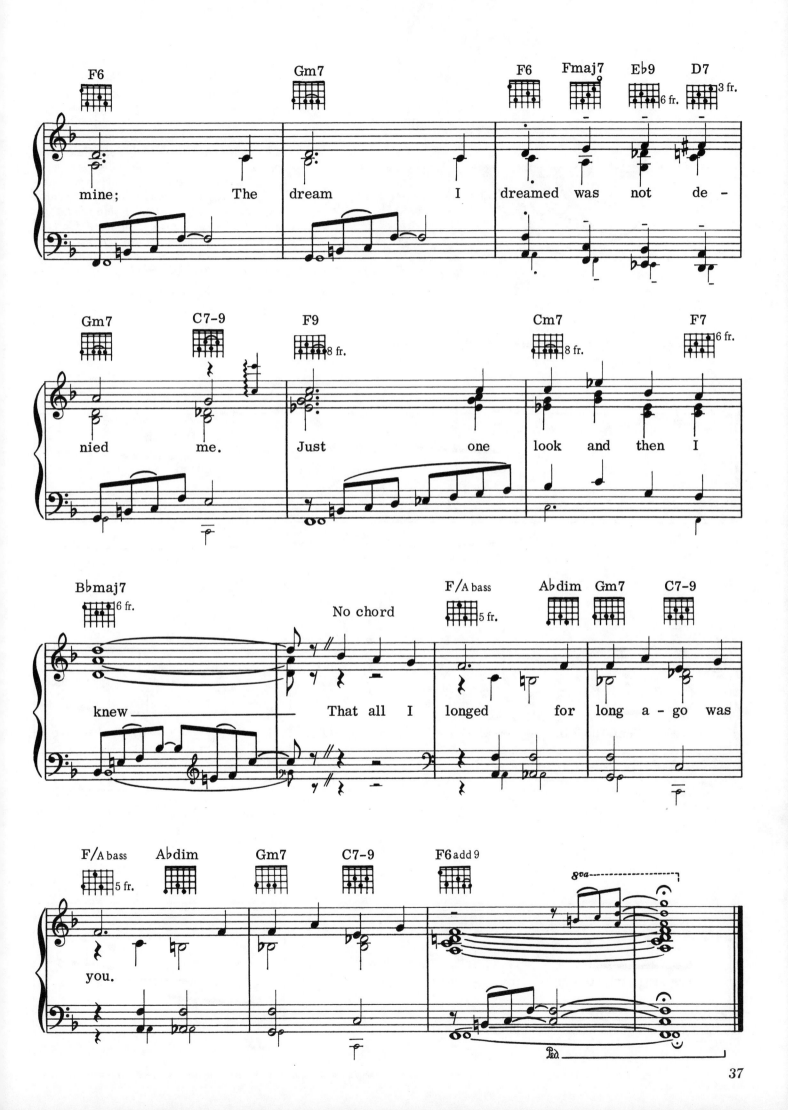

mine; The dream I dreamed was not de-

nied me. Just one look and then I

knew _____ That all I longed for long a-go was

you.

37

Gigi

from *Gigi*

The history of Gigi is strewn with celebrated names. Originally, Gigi was a novel by Colette, the French author. When the novel was turned into a play, Gigi became the first speaking role for Audrey Hepburn, who until that time had been known only as a dancer. From the stage, Gigi moved to film. The picture, which starred Leslie Caron, another former dancer, in the title role, accumulated a record-breaking total of nine Academy Awards in 1958. One of those awards was for this song, written by Alan Jay Lerner and Frederick Loewe. The score for Gigi was their first since their tremendous success with My Fair Lady in 1956. It was also their first original movie score.

Words by Alan Jay Lerner
Music by Frederick Loewe

Moderately and somewhat freely throughout

No chords

Gi - gi, am I a fool with - out a mind, Or have I

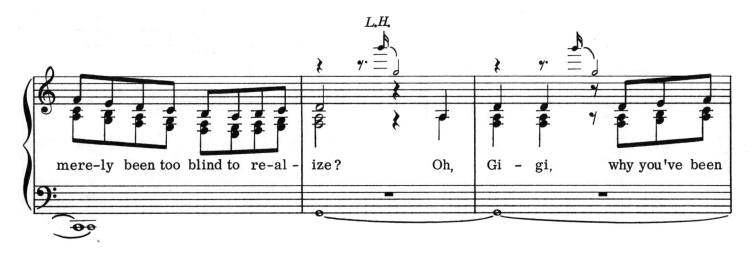

mere-ly been too blind to re-al - ize? Oh, Gi - gi, why you've been

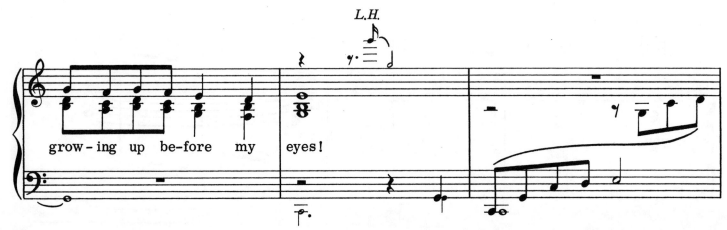

grow-ing up be-fore my eyes!

Like Johnny Mandel, who won an Academy Award for his song "The Shadow of Your Smile" in 1965, Fred Karlin was a jazz musician before he tried to scale the heights of Hollywood as a composer. A trumpeter who became an arranger for Harry James and Benny Goodman, Karlin also created music for the grand finales at Radio City Music Hall in New York. He began writing for films in 1966, and five years later lightning struck. In 1971 he won an Academy Award with the song "For All We Know," which he wrote with Robb Wilson and Arthur James, and his music for The Baby Maker *gained an Oscar nomination for the best original score. His collaborator on that musical score was the exotically named Tylwyth Kymry, a pseudonym that hid the identity of Karlin's wife, singer Meg Welles.*

For All We Know

Words by Robb Wilson and Arthur James
Music by Fred Karlin

from the motion picture *Lovers and Other Strangers*

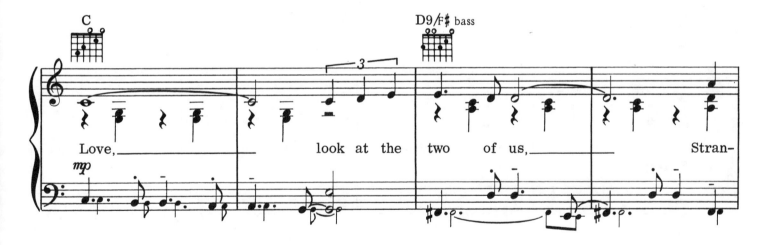

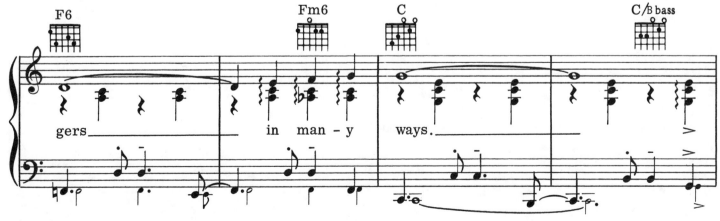

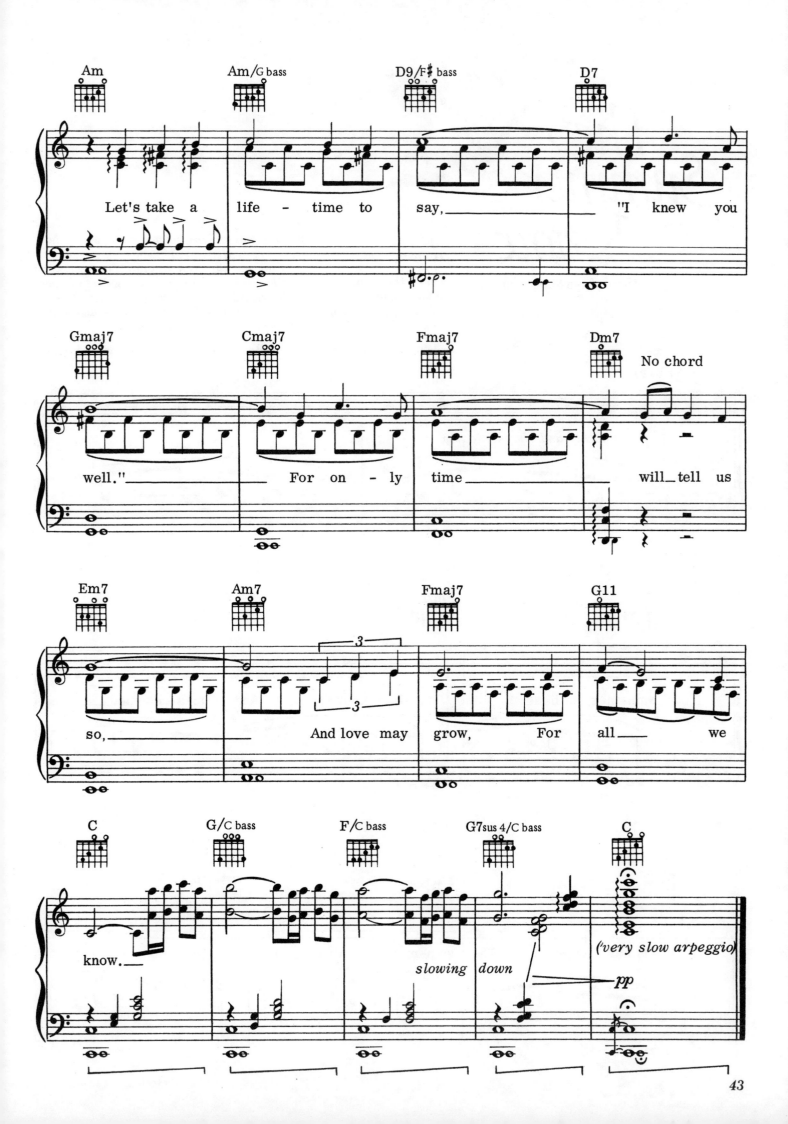

The Summer Knows

(**Theme from** *Summer of '42*)

Michel Legrand has a special talent for creating music that evokes half-forgotten memories in our minds. His jazz-influenced arrangements bring the color and flair of France to life even for those who have never been there, and the scores he composed for The Umbrellas of Cherbourg *and* The Thomas Crown Affair *reveal the qualities that add a sense of poignancy to the recollection of days of innocence and of first discoveries that are at the heart of "The Summer Knows."*

Words by Alan and Marilyn Bergman   **Music by Michel Legrand**

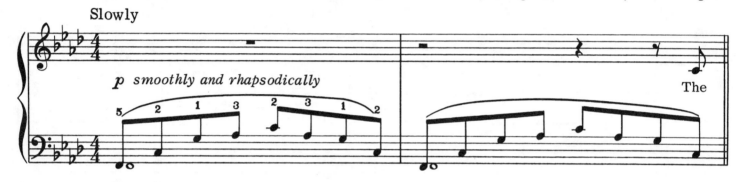

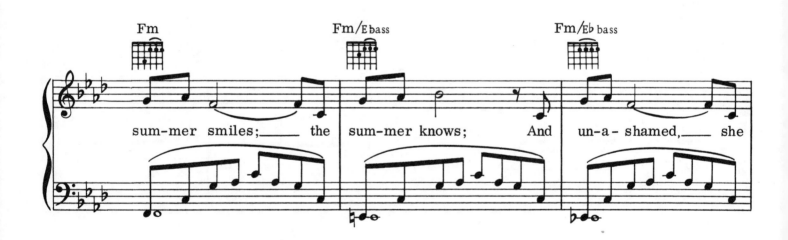

sum-mer smiles;____ the sum-mer knows; And un-a- shamed,____ she

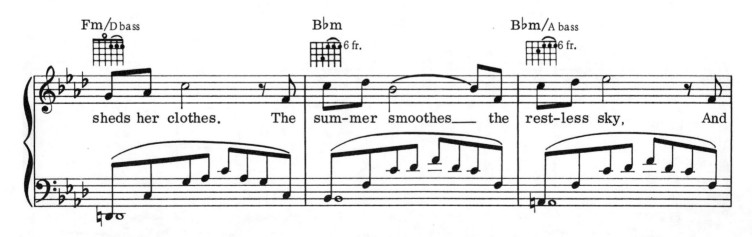

sheds her clothes. The sum-mer smoothes____ the rest-less sky, And

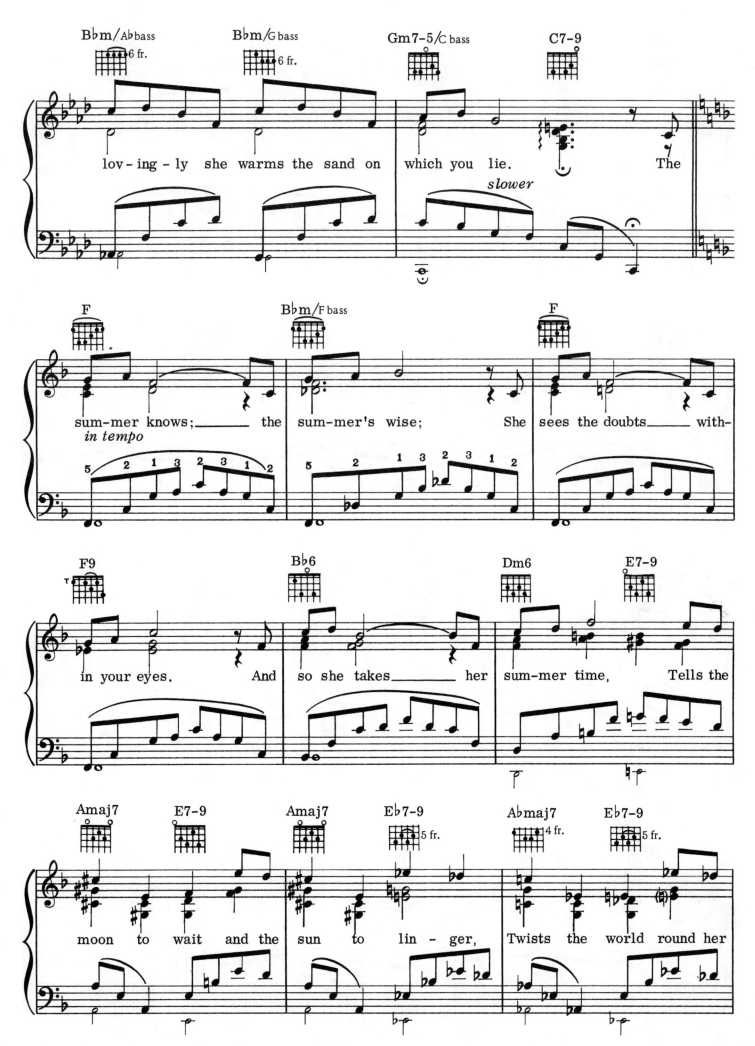

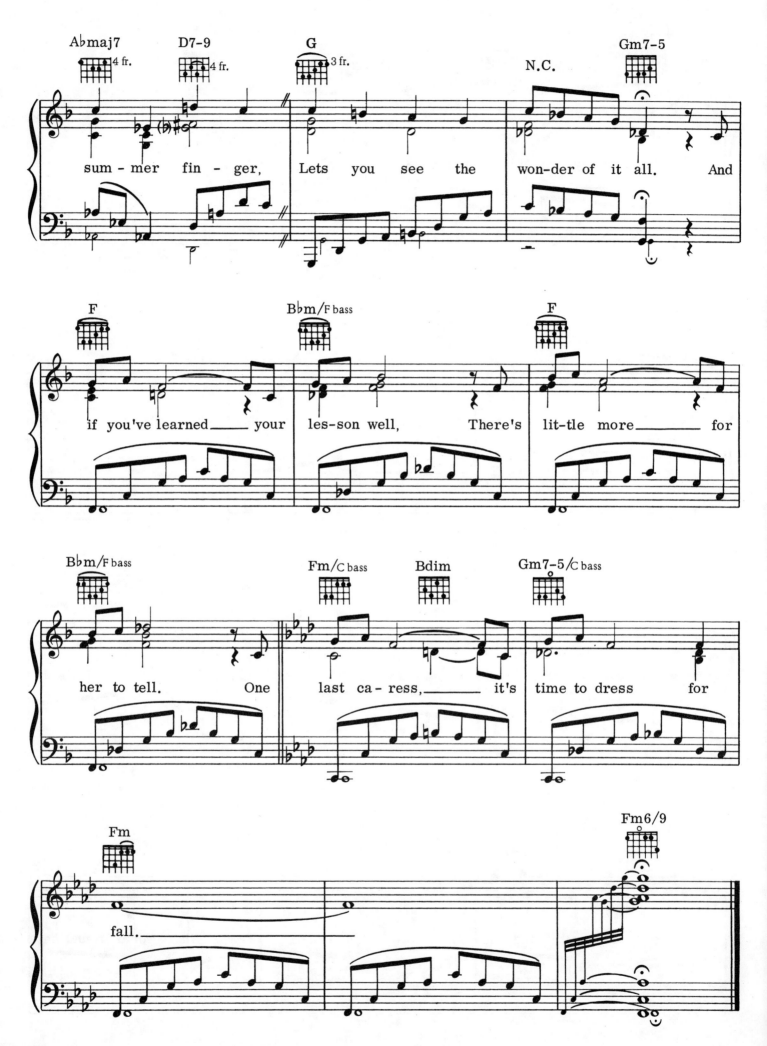

Brother, Can You Spare a Dime?

Words by E. Y. Harburg   Music by Jay Gorney

In 1932, the year of breadlines and apple sellers, most songwriters felt it their duty to cheer up America with songs like "Happy Days Are Here Again" and "Let's Have Another Cup of Coffee." But E. Y. Harburg and Jay Gorney faced the depressing facts and created "Brother, Can You Spare a Dime?," the song that became the anthem of the Depression. Harburg's lyrics reflect a personal situation. He had wanted to be a lyricist, but his friend Ira Gershwin warned him against it. It was no way to make a living, said Gershwin. So instead, Harburg started an electrical appliance business that did very well until it collapsed in the stock market crash of 1929. With a sigh of relief, Harburg returned to writing lyrics. "Brother, Can You Spare a Dime?" was in a 1932 revue called Americana.

Once I built a rail-road, made it run,__ Made it race__ a-gainst time. Once I built a rail-road; Now it's done.__

Georgia on My Mind

It was newspaper editor Stuart Gorrell, a fellow student of Hoagy Carmichael's at Indiana University, who listened to a melody that Hoagy fingered on the piano one night in 1927 and said it sounded like the dust from stars drifting down through a summer sky. So they called the song "Stardust."

And three years later it was Gorrell who wrote the lyrics for Hoagy's "Georgia on My Mind." All through the 1930's and 1940's this song was closely identified with Mildred Bailey, and more recently it has become one of the most distinctive pieces in the blues and soul repertory of Ray Charles.

Words by Stuart Gorrell **Music by Hoagy Carmichael**

Lazy River

Hoagy Carmichael thought of himself as a jazz composer when he began his songwriting career. That is, until 1929, when "Stardust," which he had written at a fast jazzy tempo, in 1927, was given a slow arrangement by Victor Young that brought out the soaring beauty of the melody. Carmichael seemed to learn something from this because his next songs— "Georgia on My Mind," "Rockin' Chair," and "Lazy River"— were slow and easy but did not lose the essential jazz and blues touch. He wrote "Lazy River" in collaboration with Sidney Arodin, a New Orleans clarinetist, and the warm, gentle flow of its melody comes from the relaxed, easygoing sound that was typical of New Orleans' great clarinetists.

**Words and music by
Hoagy Carmichael and Sidney Arodin**

In a lazy 4

Up a la-zy riv-er by the old mill run, That la-zy, la-zy riv-er in the noon-day sun, Lin-ger in the shade of a kind old tree; Throw a-way your trou-bles, dream a dream with me.—

I Don't Know Why

Fred Ahlert went to Fordham Law School before he turned to music (as an arranger for Irving Aaronson's Commanders), and Roy Turk switched from studying architecture at the College of the City of New York to writing special material for Nora Bayes and Sophie Tucker. The quondam lawyer and would-be architect became a songwriting team in 1928, and they hit the jackpot with their first song—"I'll Get By." Until

Turk's death in 1934, they turned out a consistent stream of songs that have become pop classics—"Mean to Me," "Walkin' My Baby Back Home," "Where the Blue of the Night (Meets the Gold of the Day)," and "I Don't Know Why (I Just Do)." Ahlert collaborated with other lyricists after his partner died, composing "I'm Gonna Sit Right Down and Write Myself a Letter" and "The Moon Was Yellow" among others.

Words by Roy Turk

Music by Fred E. Ahlert

*It is very important to play this arrangement softly.

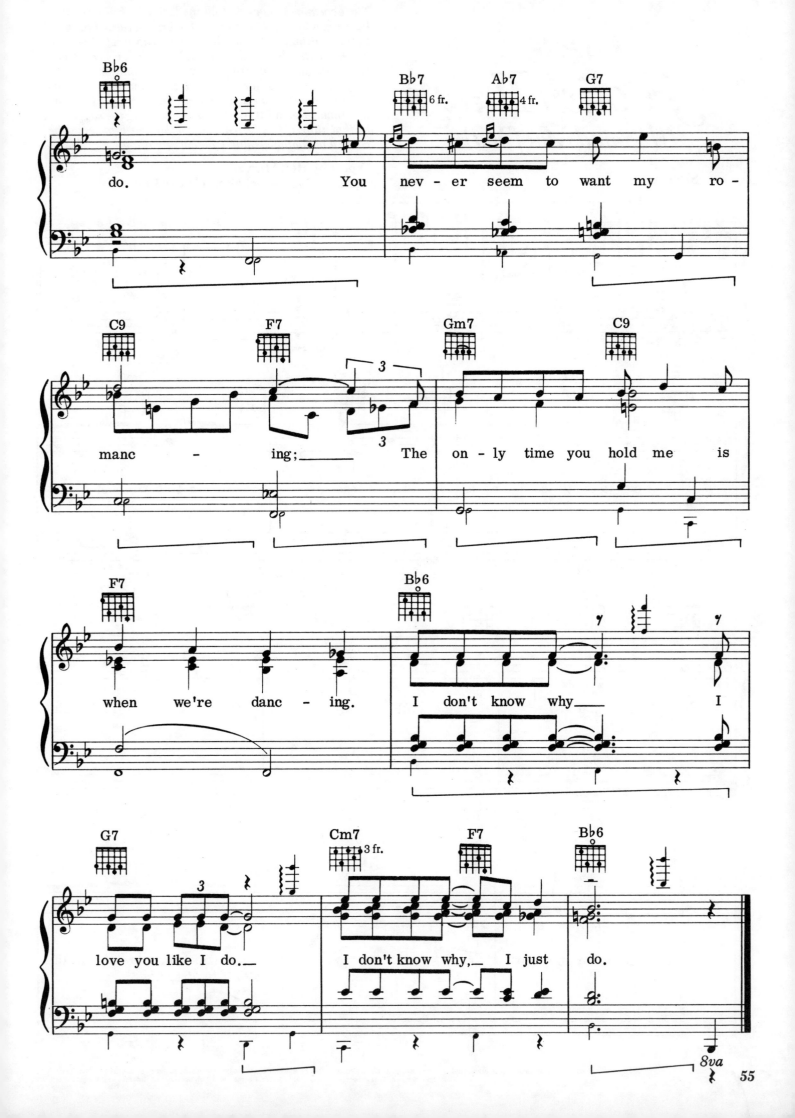

These Foolish Things
(Remind Me of You)

The evocative images that fill the lyrics of this song might have been the work of a poet who, briefly, turned his hand to songwriting. But Eric Maschwitz, who wrote the lyrics in 1935 under the pseudonym Holt Marvell, was an executive with the British Broadcasting Corporation, and the song was created for a special BBC musical program. "These Foolish Things" turned up the next year in a London revue, Spread It Abroad, and following the suggestion of that title, it finally reached the United States and became a memorable Billie Holiday recording.

Words by Holt Marvell
Music by Jack Strachey and Harry Link

Slowly

It's Only a Paper Moon

The 1932 nonmusical The Great Magoo included a song called "If You Believed in Me" that has lasted through the years. But you wouldn't recognize it by that name because, when it was sung a year later by Buddy Rogers and June Knight in the film Take a Chance, it had been retitled "It's Only a Paper Moon." People tend to remember only a song's opening words, and the original title was buried inside lyrics that begin, "It's only a paper moon." That's why "If You Believed in Me" flopped, but "It's Only a Paper Moon" became a hit.

Words by Billy Rose and E. Y. Harburg
Music by Harold Arlen

Moderate swing

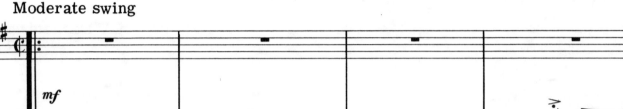

Say, it's on-ly a pa-per moon,___ Sail-ing o-ver a

card-board sea,___ But it would-n't be make-be-lieve___ If you___

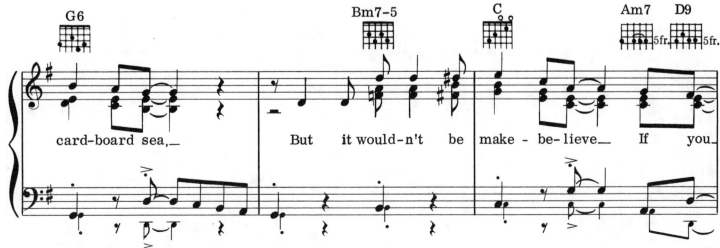

rade; With-out your love, it's a mel-o-dy played in a slower - - -

pen-ny ar-cade. *a tempo* It's a Bar-num and Bai-ley world,_

Just as phon-y as it can be,_ But it would-n't be make-be-lieve_ If

you be - lieved in me.

Solitude

Words by Eddie De Lange and Irving Mills
Music by Duke Ellington

With "Solitude," composer Duke Ellington emerged from the shadowy, exotic jazz world into the world of pop songs. "Solitude," written in 1933, was Ellington's first popular hit; and like most of his music, it was written quickly, on the spur of the moment. He was in a recording studio in Chicago with his band waiting for another band to finish using the studio. The Duke used the time to jot down the tune, writing it on a piece of paper held against a wall.

Love Letters in the Sand

For more than 30 years Nick Kenny wrote what ostensibly was a radio and TV column for the New York Daily Mirror. The column often gave more prominence to Kenny's own sentimental poems and birthday greetings to friends than it did to airwave activities. One day in 1931 composer J. Fred Coots came across Kenny's poem "Love Letters in the Sand" in the column and set it to music. Russ Columbo recorded the song, but the big push came when George Hall, whose orchestra broadcast every day from the Hotel Taft in New York, made it his theme song. Pat Boone's 1957 recording of "Love Letters" sold more than a million copies.

Slowly in 2 (♩ = 1 beat)

Words by Nick and Charles Kenny   Music by J. Fred Coots

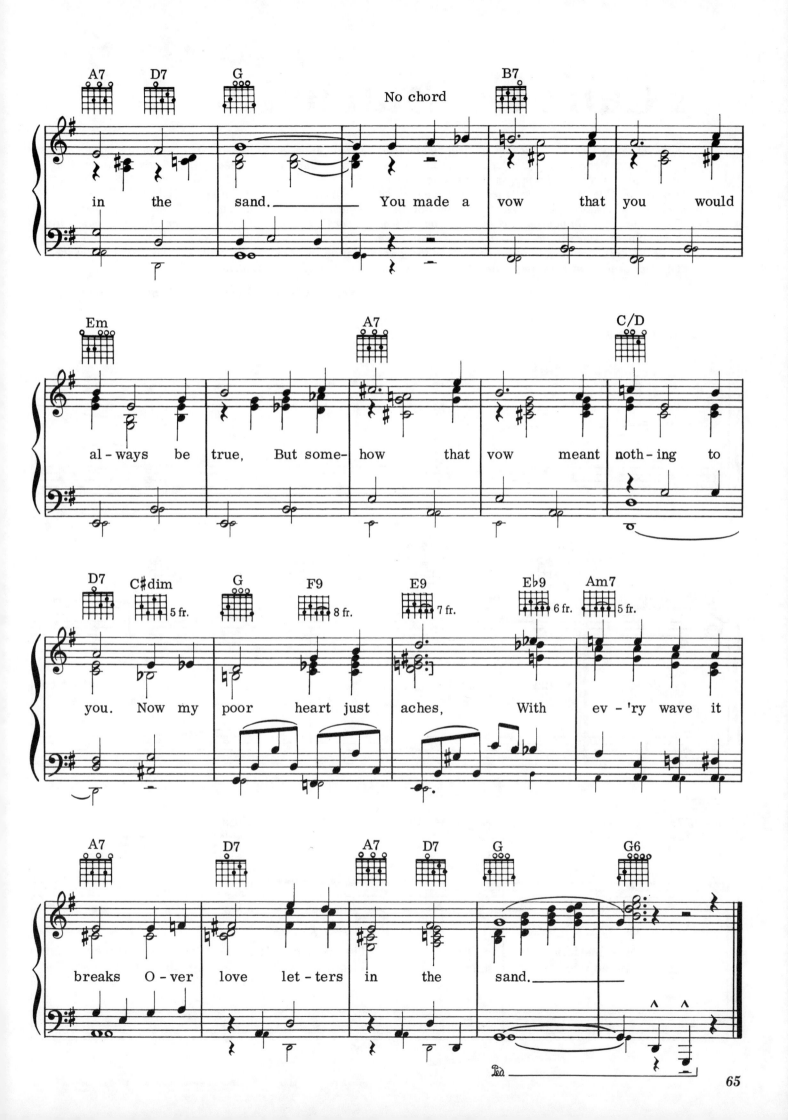

I Can't Get Started

In 1933 George Gershwin became completely involved in Porgy and Bess, leaving Ira, for the first time in almost 10 years, with time for projects that did not involve his brother. One of the projects was a score which he wrote with Vernon Duke for Ziegfeld Follies of 1936. The Follies, a posthumous use of Ziegfeld's name, was in the lavish, star-studded (Fanny Brice, Josephine Baker, Bobby Clark, Gypsy Rose Lee) style of the great "Glorifier of the American Girl." But it was not as suc- cessful as earlier Follies—the only memory it left behind was "I Can't Get Started," sung in the show by Bob Hope and Eve Arden. In 1937 Bunny Berigan, a jazz trumpeter, made a recording of "I Can't Get Started" on which he ventured to sing as well as play trumpet. The recording proved to be one of the classics of jazz improvisation and demonstrated how a jazz musician, who was not really a singer, could use his instrumental talents to direct his vocalizing.

Words by Ira Gershwin   Music by Vernon Duke

Moderately slow

I've flown a-round the world in a plane; I've set-tled
hun-dred yards in ten flat; The Prince of

rev - o - lu-tions in Spain; The North Pole I have chart-ed, But
Wales has cop-ied my hat; With queens I've à la cart-ed, But

Winter Wonderland

Felix Bernard, who wrote the melody of "Winter Wonderland," is also credited as a composer of "Dardanella," a big hit of 1919. "Dardanella" had supposedly originated as a piano rag by Johnny S. Black (who also wrote "Paper Doll"), with lyrics by Fred Fisher. However, when Bernard, a vaudeville performer, produced evidence that he had written the basic melody and had given it to Johnny Black, Fisher paid him $100 for his interest in the piece. Then, when the song became a tremendous hit, Bernard sued Fisher, claiming he had been duped. Bernard lost the suit but in 1934 came up with a much better annuity in "Winter Wonderland," a piece that is played regularly every Christmas while "Dardanella" has been reduced to a nostalgic novelty tune.

Words by Dick Smith   Music by Felix Bernard

Johnny Mercer was just starting out as a songwriter when he wrote "Goody-Goody" with Matt Malneck in 1936. Both of them were with Paul Whiteman's band at the time, Mercer as a singer, Malneck as a violinist. "Between sets at the Biltmore Hotel in New York," he recalled, "we used to sit down and write songs. Benny Goodman was a good friend, and after he started his band, I played some of my songs for him." The first Mercer song that Benny recorded was "The Dixieland Band." The next one was "Goody-Goody." On the strength of the popularity of "Goody-Goody," Mercer got a contract to write for the movies—and he stayed in California until his death in 1976.

Words and music by Johnny Mercer and Matt Malneck

74

section 3: Top Tunes of the 1940s

I'll Be Seeing You

With its heart-tugging images of memories brought about by separation, "I'll Be Seeing You" touched a responsive chord in war-weary Americans. It had been written in 1938 by the songwriting team of Sammy Fain and Irving Kahal for an unsuccessful Broadway musical, Right This Way, in which it was sung by the sultry Russian singer Tamara. A few years later Hildegarde, another "Continental" chanteuse (although she came from Milwaukee), got the song started, and Frank Sinatra lifted it to the number one spot on the Hit Parade in 1944.

Words by Irving Kahal   **Music by Sammy Fain**

small ca - fé, The park a - cross the way, The

chil - dren's car - ou - sel, The chest - nut trees, the

wish - ing well. I'll be see - ing you In

ev - 'ry love - ly sum - mer's day, In ev - 'ry-thing that's
gradually getting louder and more intense

Blueberry Hill

"Blueberry Hill" was the product of three of the more successful hands in Tin Pan Alley—Vincent Rose, who also wrote "Avalon," "Whispering," and "Linger Awhile"; Al Lewis, writer of "The Breeze," "Now's the Time to Fall in Love," and "Rose O'Day"; and Larry Stock, who composed "You're Nobody Till Somebody Loves You" and "You Won't Be Satisfied." They wrote "Blueberry Hill" for Gene Autry to sing in the 1941 film The Singing Hills. But it was Glenn Miller's recording of "Blueberry Hill," with a vocal by Ray Eberle, that put the song on the Hit Parade that year. In 1949 it was picked up by Louis Armstrong when he was reviving his jazz career with The All-Stars and his record company was trying to get him back into the pop field by recording him with Gordon Jenkins' orchestra. "Blueberry Hill" did it for him then, and even after Fats Domino gave the song a third revival in 1957, Armstrong continued to rely on it as a big number until his death in 1971.

Words and music by Al Lewis, Larry Stock, and Vincent Rose

79

Don't Sit Under the Apple Tree
(With Anyone Else But Me)

Words by Lew Brown and Charlie Tobias   Music by Sam H. Stept

"Don't Sit Under the Apple Tree" began its career in the mid-thirties as a melody by Sam Stept, a veteran writer of such pop songs as "That's My Weakness Now," "I'll Always Be in Love with You," and "Please Don't Talk About Me When I'm Gone." He called his tune "Anywhere the Bluebird Goes." Lew Brown and Charlie Tobias later wrote lyrics for it and, as "Don't Sit Under the Apple Tree (With Anyone Else But Me)," it was worked into the score of the 1939 Broadway musical Yokel Boy. Three years later the Andrews Sisters sang it in a movie, Private Buckaroo, and it became one of the first of the World War II hits. For the departing GI's it was an appeal to their girls at home to be faithful.

There'll Be Bluebirds Over The White Cliffs of Dover

Words by Nat Burton
Music by Walter Kent

In the dark days of 1941, the high, white chalk cliffs of Dover on the English Channel coast were guideposts for the German planes that flew in a seemingly endless stream to bomb London and other inland targets. At the height of the Battle of Britain, the skies above the cliffs held only terror for the British and their Allies. But Nat Burton and Walter Kent, two American songwriters, looked ahead to better days, when the bombers would be replaced by blue-birds, and created one of the most touching of the "stiff upper lip" songs to come out of World War II.

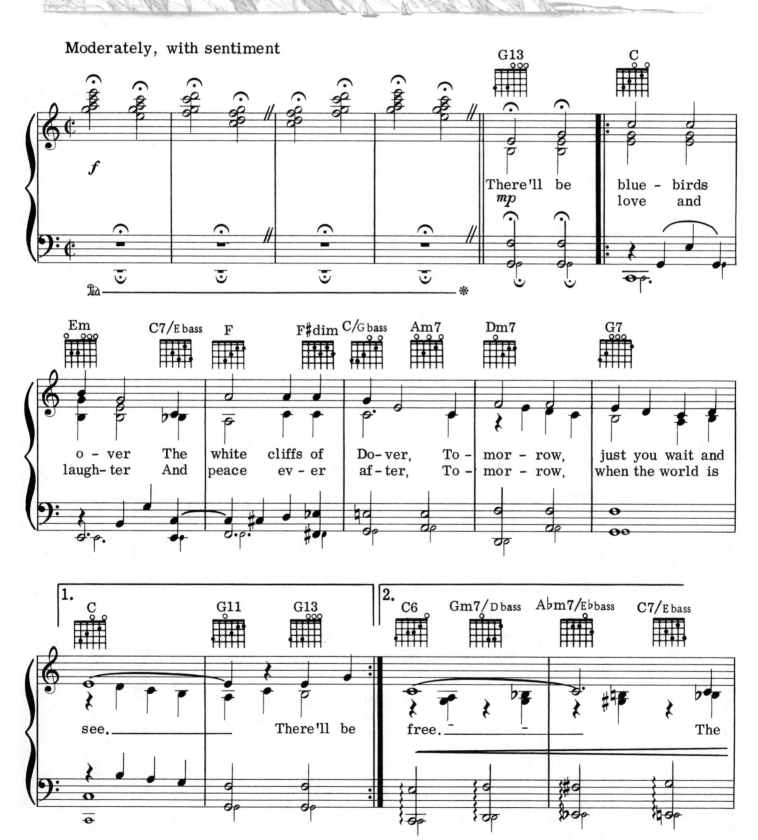

shep-herd will tend his sheep; The val-ley will bloom a- gain; And

Jim-my will go to sleep In his own lit-tle room a- gain. There'll be

blue - birds o - ver The white cliffs of Do - ver, To-

mor - row, just you wait and see.

(Aquellos Ojos Verdes)
Green Eyes

Moderate Latin feeling

mf

C

Your green eyes with their soft lights,
A - que - llos o - jos ver - des

Your eyes that prom-ise
de mi - ra - da se-

sweet nights
re - na,

Bring to my soul a long - ing,
De - ja - ron en mi al - ma

C#dim

G7

A thirst for love di - vine.
eter - na sed de a - mar,

In dreams I seem to
An - he - los de ca-

Most Americans remember "Green Eyes" as the prototype of the Bob Eberly-Helen O'Connell duets, with Jimmy Dorsey's orchestra, that were very popular in the 1940's. But this Cuban tune, composed by Nilo Menéndez, had its original success early in the thirties as part of the first invasion of Latin American dance music into North America. When Jimmy Dorsey gave the song to his two singers, they found that Helen did not have the range to cover the bottom-to-top pick-up notes that carried the words "those cool and limpid green eyes." She faked it by turning the words into a Mae-West-like exclamation. "It killed the listeners," says Eberly, "and that's what made the song."

English translation by E. Rivera and E. Woods

Original Spanish words by Adolfo Utrera

Music by Nilo Menéndez

What a Diff'rence a Day Made

(Cuando Vuelva a Tu Lado)

Ironically, "What a Diff'rence a Day Made," known now primarily through Dinah Washington's strong 1959 "soul" version, had a Latin rhythm when it first became popular in Mexico in the 1930's. Then it was called "Cuando Vuelva a Tu Lado." It became a hit in North America only after Stanley Adams wrote the English lyrics that made it "What a Diff'rence a Day Made." Maria Grever, who wrote the original words and music, was a violinist, pianist, and concert singer before she turned to writing pop songs, which also included "Ti-Pi-Tin," "Magic Is the Moonlight," and "Lamento Gitano," an instrumental number popularized by Stan Kenton.

English words by Stanley Adams
Music and Spanish words by Maria Grever

Moderate Latin tempo

Now Is the Hour

(Maori Farewell Song)

Most of the popular songs that grew out of World War II came from the European side of the battle. One of the very few that reached us from the Pacific was "Now Is the Hour," a song of the Maoris of New Zealand, originally known as "Maori Farewell Song." It was given English lyrics and its English title, and Gracie Fields, the great British music-hall entertainer, popularized it during the last stages of the war. This was a period when the conflict in Europe was drawing to an end and attention was being riveted on the Pacific. When the war ended with the surrender of the Japanese in August 1945, there were hundreds of thousands of servicemen for whom the plaintive strains of "Now Is the Hour" had a very emotional tug.

Original words by Maewae Kaihau   Music by Clement Scott
English words by Dorothy Stewart

Now is the hour_____ When we must say good-
Te   i - wi   te   I - wi   e   te   i - wi

bye._____ Soon you'll be sail - ing
e;   Ta   hu - ri   mai   ra

Haere ra
Te manu tangi pai;
E haere ana,
Koe ki pamamao.
Haere ra,
Ka hoki mai ano,
Kite tau
E tangi atu nei.

Polka Dots and Moonbeams

In the late thirties, Jimmy Van Heusen, working as a piano player for a New York music publisher, often collaborated on songs with visitors to the office. One day in 1939, lyricist Johnny Burke, who, with James V. Monaco, had been writing songs for Bing Crosby, "just came into the office to shoot the breeze," Van Heusen recalled. "He said to me, 'You got any tunes?' I said, 'Sure.' So we went out and wrote 'Oh, You Crazy Moon.' The next time he came in, we did 'Polka Dots and Moonbeams.'" It was the beginning of a tremendously successful songwriting team that lasted more than 15 years.

Words by Johnny Burke   Music by Jimmy Van Heusen

You Made Me Love You
(I Didn't Want To Do It)

Al Jolson introduced "You Made Me Love You" in The Honeymoon Express *in 1913. The show marked the first time he appeared in blackface, and the song established another trademark: While singing it, he got down on one knee and stretched out his arms. He did this simply to relieve the pressure on a very painful ingrown toenail. A quarter of a century later 15-year-old Judy Garland sang the song to a photograph of Clark Gable in* Broadway Melody of 1938, *which launched her film career. And in 1941 Harry James had his first big hit as a bandleader with "You Made Me Love You," copying Judy's vocal inflections on his trumpet because he liked the way she sang the song.*

Words by Joe McCarthy   Music by James V. Monaco

Moderately

You made me love you. I did-n't want to do it; I did-n't want to do it.

You made me want you, And all the time you knew it; I guess you al-ways knew it.

Peg O' My Heart

One of the earliest "title" songs—common-place in present-day movies—was "Peg o' My Heart," written in 1913 by Fred Fisher and Alfred Bryan and inspired by the play Peg o' My Heart, which starred Laurette Taylor. The song had no relationship whatever to the play or its characters. It was introduced and popularized in the Ziegfeld Follies of 1913 by Jose Collins, one of the most popular singers of the day. However, the cover of the sheet music carried a picture of Miss Taylor, whose performance in Peg o' My Heart made her even more popular than Miss Collins. Although the song has been a sentimental favorite ever since, it reached a new peak of popularity in 1947 due to a recording by a harmonica ensemble called Jerry Murad's Harmonicats.

Words by Alfred Bryan   Music by Fred Fisher

With a Gaelic lilt

mp freely

held back

Cmaj7   D9

Peg o' my heart,___ I love you; We'll nev-er part,___
in tempo

G11

___ I love you. Dear lit-tle girl,___ sweet lit-tle girl,___

It's a Long, Long Way to Tipperary

Words and music by Jack Judge and Harry Williams

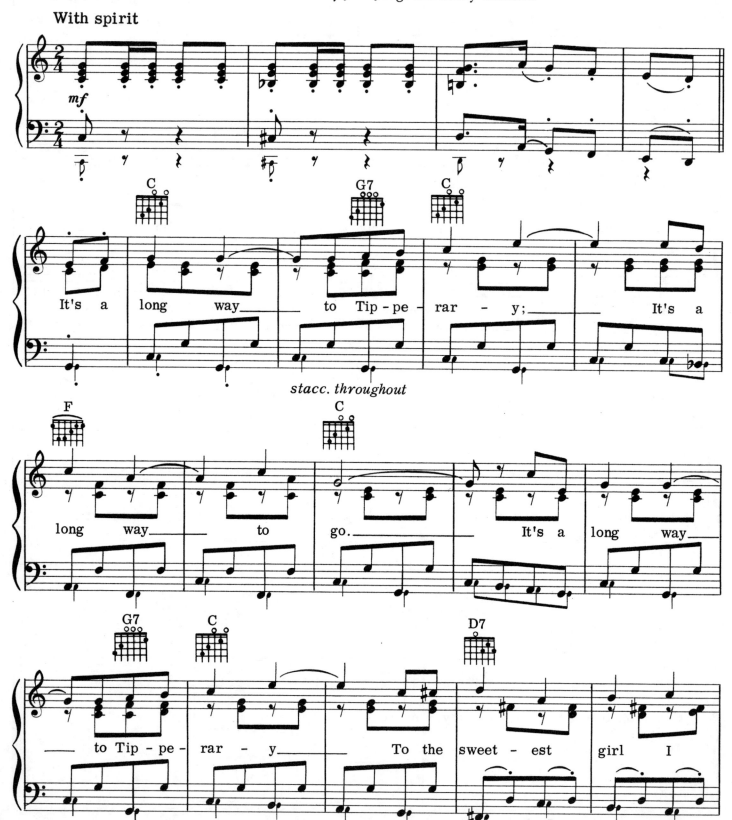

With spirit

It's a long way to Tip-pe-rar-y; It's a long way to go. It's a long way to Tip-pe-rar-y To the sweet-est girl I

Before the United States became involved in World War I, Americans were singing "I Didn't Raise My Boy to Be a Soldier" and "Don't Take My Darling Boy Away," while the English, who were already fighting, sang "Keep the Home Fires Burning," "Pack Up Your Troubles in Your Old Kit Bag," and "It's a Long, Long Way to Tipperary." Americans took to the English songs, too, even though they may not have known where or what Tipperary was (it is a dairy town in County Tipperary in the south of Ireland). "It's a Long, Long Way" was written in 1912 by a pair of English vaudevillians, Jack Judge and Harry Williams. (Judge may have written it himself and "cut" Williams in on the royalties as a means of repaying a loan.) They wrote it as a love ballad, but during the war the soldiers adopted it as a marching tune.

How Ya Gonna Keep 'em Down on the Farm?
(After They've Seen Paree)

"How Ya Gonna Keep 'em Down on the Farm?" was written in 1919, the year following the Armistice that ended World War I. The idea of doughboys having such
a good time in Gay Paree that they would never again settle for the drudgery of
farm life presaged the overall change in moral standards that followed the war and
turned the 1920's into "The Jazz Age." The song's composer, Walter Donaldson,
went on to write "My Buddy," "Carolina in the Morning," "My Blue Heaven," "Love
Me or Leave Me," "Yes Sir, That's My Baby," and many others.

Words by Sam M. Lewis and Joe Young   Music by Walter Donaldson

Moderately bright

How ya gon-na keep 'em down on the farm___ Af-ter they've seen___ Pa-ree?___ How ya gon-na keep 'em a-way from Broad-way, Jazz-in' a-roun'___ and paint-in' the town?

How ya gon-na keep 'em a- way from harm? That's a mys-ter-

y. They'll nev- er want to see a rake or plow,

And who the deuce can par- ley- voo a cow? How ya gon-na keep 'em

down on the farm After they've seen Pa - ree?

Down by the Old Mill Stream

In the first decade of the 20th century the saccharine songs of the 1890's had given way to slightly more realistic lyrics, but barbershop quartets were still harmonizing valiantly. A song that allowed for the closest possible harmony as well as physical expression was bound to be a favorite. "Down by the Old Mill Stream" fulfilled both qualifica- tions to such an extent that, along with "Sweet Adeline," it remains today at the top of the four-part harmony list. In the forties The Mills Brothers gave it an added lease on life when they swung it into their harmonized jazz context. Tell Taylor, who wrote it, spent his lifetime as a songwriter, but this was the only one of his songs that became a hit.

Words and music by Tell Taylor

The Missouri Waltz
Song

Words by James R. Shannon   **Music by John Valentine Eppel**
Adapted by Frederic Knight Logan

Even if Harry Truman had not been a piano-playing president from Missouri, "The Missouri Waltz" would probably still be remembered and played today. Frederic Knight Logan, a composer and musical director from Oskaloosa, Iowa, arranged and published it as a piano piece in 1914. But the song had been written a few years earlier by John Valentine Eppel, a sometime railroad man who was also a composer and bandleader. A year after the song's publication, James R. Shannon, composer of "Too-Ra-Loo-Ra-Loo-Ral," added the lyrics of a lullaby. It is now Missouri's state song.

Slow and dreamy

Hush - a–bye, my ba - by, Slum - ber - time__ is com - in' soon;

Rest__ your head up - on__ my breast While Mom - my hums a tune. The

sand-man is call - in' Where shad-ows are fall-in', While the soft breez-es

You're a Grand Old Flag

In his third musical, the 1906 George Washington, Jr., George M. Cohan, the great musical flag-waver, draped himself in an American flag as he danced and sang a song in its honor. Cohan got the idea for the song, which came to be known as "You're a Grand Old Flag," from a Civil War veteran who had been a Union colorbearer. Of the flag he had carried then, the old man said to Cohan, "She's a grand old rag." Cohan liked the warmth of the phrase and wrote the song as "You're a Grand Old Rag." But after he sang it in the show, he was denounced by patriotic societies, who accused him of insulting the American flag. So he changed "rag" to "flag," and his standing as a patriot was cleared.

Words and music by George M. Cohan

Oh Johnny, Oh Johnny, Oh!

Abe Olman, a successful music publisher, got his basic training when he became a song plugger for a song he wrote in 1917, "Oh Johnny, Oh Johnny, Oh!" He got an imposing list of stars to sing it—Al Jolson, Eddie Cantor, Sophie Tucker, Ted Lewis—and it was featured in a Ziegfeld Follies. It became one of the big hits of World War I, selling 1¼ million copies of sheet music. By the time Wee Bonnie Baker repopularized it in 1939, piping it out in a little-girl voice, with Orrin Tucker's orchestra, record sales rather than sheet music had become the barometer of success, but even on records "Oh Johnny" was a million-seller.

Moderately

Words by Ed Rose Music by Abe Olman

Oh, John-ny! Oh, John-ny! How you can love!___ Oh, John-ny!

Oh, John-ny! Heav-ens a-bove!___ You make my sad heart jump with

joy,___ And when you're near I just can't Sit still a

section 5: The Sunny, Funny 1920s

Toot, Toot, Tootsie!
(Good-bye)

When you realize that the plot of Bombo, in which Al Jolson starred in 1921, focused on a black deckhand who helps Christopher Columbus discover America, you can understand why Jolson kept inserting new songs into the show to take the audience's mind off the book. One of the songs was "Toot, Toot, Tootsie! Good-bye," composed by bandleaders Dan Russo and Ted Fiorito, with lyrics by the ubiquitous Gus Kahn and Ernie Erdman, a lyricist and pianist in the Original New Orleans Jazz Band. Sigmund Romberg's score for Bombo was quickly forgotten, but Jolson's interpolated songs became some of his greatest hits. In addition to "Toot, Toot, Tootsie," they included "California, Here I Come" and "April Showers."

Words and music by Gus Kahn, Ernie Erdman, Dan Russo, and Ted Fiorito

Watch for the mail;____ I'll nev-er fail;____ If

you don't get a let-ter, Then you'll know I'm in jail.____

Tut, tut, toot-sie, don't cry.____

Toot, toot, toot-sie, good-bye.____

8va lower

When the Red, Red Robin Comes Bob, Bob, Bobbin' Along

When Harry Woods wrote "When the Red, Red Robin Comes Bob, Bob, Bobbin' Along," he was trying to make a living as a farmer on Cape Cod. This song, which Sophie Tucker introduced in Chicago in 1926, got Woods off the land and into the Brill Building, the locus for songwriters in New York City. A year later Woods and his bride, Barbara, were settled in an apartment in New York but were having a hard time making ends meet. This inspired him to write "Side by Side," a hit that helped their financial situation. It was followed by such Woods hits as "I'm Looking Over a Four-Leaf Clover," "When the Moon Comes Over the Mountain," "River, Stay 'Way From My Door," and "Try a Little Tenderness."

Words and music by Harry Woods

Wake up, wake up, you sleep-y-head; Get up, get up, get out___ of bed; Cheer up, cheer up, the sun___ is red; Live, love, laugh, and be hap-py. What if I've been blue Now I'm walk-in' through fields of flow'rs.

Sunny Side Up

In 1929 Buddy DeSylva, Lew Brown, and Ray Henderson headed for Hollywood to write songs for one of the earliest movie musicals, *Sunny Side Up,* which starred Charles Farrell and Janet Gaynor. The title song they wrote became one of the first and most successful "keep your chin up" songs of the subsequent Depression. DeSylva, Brown, and Henderson proved to be as successful at writing for films as they had been at composing for the stage. In addition to this song, their score for *Sunny Side Up* included "I'm a Dreamer, Aren't We All?" "Turn on the Heat," and, a valentine to Hollywood, "If I Had a Talking Picture of You."

**Words and music by B. G. DeSylva,
Lew Brown, and Ray Henderson**

Moderately in 2 (♩ = 1 beat)

Keep your sun - ny side up, up! Hide the side that gets blue. If you have nine sons in a row, Base - ball teams make

mon- ey, you know! ___ Keep your fun - ny side up,

up! Let your laugh - ter come through,

do! Stand up on ___ your legs; Be like two___

___ fried eggs; Keep your sun - ny side up!

You're the Cream in My Coffee

Moderate bounce

You're the cream in my cof - fee;
You're the starch in my col - lar,
You're the salt_ in my
You're the lace_ in my
stew.
shoe.
You will al - ways be
my ne-ces-si-ty;
I'd be lost_ with-out you.
Most men_ tell
love tales_
And each phrase dove - tails_
You've heard_ each

DeSylva, Brown, and Henderson's satire on the boxing business and "clean sportsmanship"—the 1928 musical Hold Everything—gave Bert Lahr, a veteran of burlesque and vaudeville, his first role in a Broadway "book" show. His tremendous success as a punch-drunk prizefighter launched a long career that lifted him from slapstick comedy to such dramatic roles as Estragon in Waiting for Godot. *The bright and topical score was topped by "You're the Cream in My Coffee," sung by Jack Whiting. The song turned up in the 1929 film* The Cockeyed World, *a follow-up to* What Price Glory? *that also starred Victor McLaglen and Edmund Lowe.*

Words and music by B. G. DeSylva, Lew Brown, and Ray Henderson

Button Up Your Overcoat

The highly successful songwriting team of lyricists Buddy De-Sylva and Lew Brown and composer Ray Henderson was formed when Henderson was brought in to compose the score for George White's Scandals of 1925. In addition to Scandals scores from 1925 to 1928, DeSylva, Brown, and Henderson did scores for a series of musical comedies that satirized the mores of the late twenties—rah-rah college life in the 1927 Good News, boxing in 1928 in Hold Everything, and golf in the 1929 Follow Thru. "Button Up Your Overcoat" appeared in Follow Thru, sung by Jack Haley and Zelma O'Neal. With its listing of "do's" and "don'ts," current fads and old wives' tales, it has the kind of topical humor on which Cole Porter also prospered.

Words and music by B. G. DeSylva, Lew Brown, and Ray Henderson

Diane

from the William Fox production *Seventh Heaven*

In 1926, when the silent film version of *What Price Glory?* was made with Victor McLaglen, Edmund Lowe, and Dolores Del Rio, composer Erno Rapée was commissioned to write a tune that could be used to advertise the film. With lyricist Lew Pollack, he wrote "Charmaine," named for the Dolores Del Rio character. Since the movie had no soundtrack, "Charmaine" was not actually heard as part of the film presentation. But the response to the song was so great and the benefit of having a popular song associated with a film so evident that the following year, when Hollywood first began using sound, Rapée and Pollack were asked to write a song that would actually be heard in a film. The film was *Seventh Heaven* with Janet Gaynor and Charles Farrell, and the song was "Diane," sung on the soundtrack by an unseen, unidentified female vocalist. It was one of the first and most popular modern movie theme songs.

Words and music by Erno Rapée and Lew Pollack

If You Knew Susie
(Like I Know Susie)

"If You Knew Susie" was originally written for Al Jolson by Buddy DeSylva and Joseph Meyer. Jolson sang it in his 1925 show Big Boy, but even though he was at the peak of his success, the song got little reaction. So Jolson gave it to Eddie Cantor and told him, "I think this would fit you better than it does me." When Cantor first sang it at a benefit show in his typical anxious, jumping manner, patting his hands together and popping his eyes, he brought down the house. Jolson, who was on the same program, later said to Cantor, "Eddie, you dirty dog, if I'd known the song was that good, I'd never have given it to you." It was a marvelous gift: "If You Knew Susie" was identified with Cantor for the rest of his career.

Words and music by B. G. DeSylva and Joseph Meyer

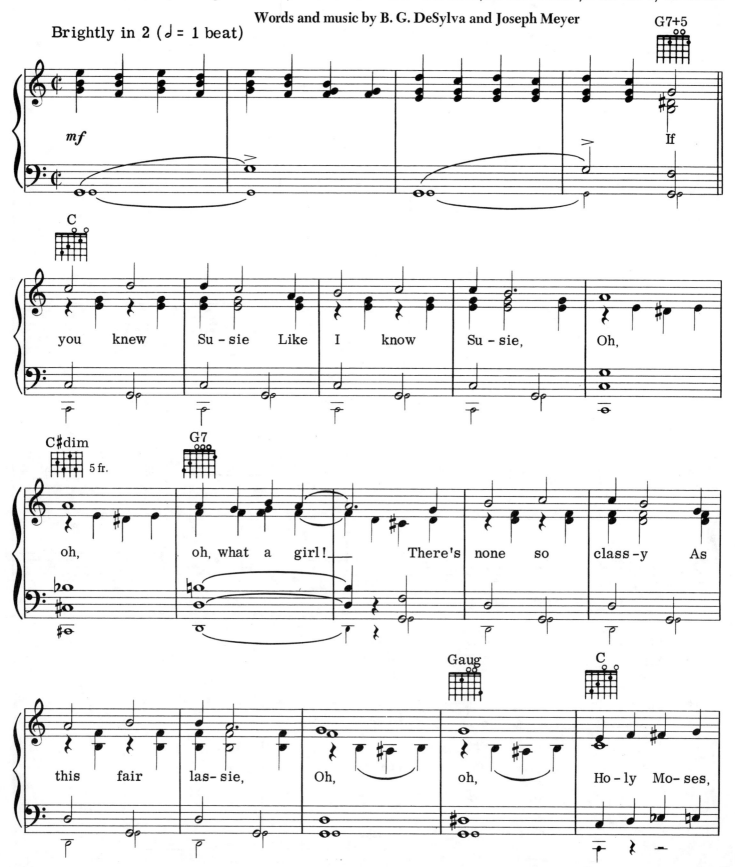

Sweet Lorraine

Cliff Burwell had just joined Rudy Vallee's band as a pianist when he composed "Sweet Lorraine" in 1928. Although Vallee and his Connecticut Yankees had turned many songs into hits, "Sweet Lorraine" was not one of them. A variety of radio and vaudeville performers sang it successfully before Nat "King" Cole put his personal stamp on it in 1937 in a performance that changed his career. At that time Cole was a nonsinging pianist whose trio was playing in a Los Angeles club, the Swanee Inn. A drunken customer there kept insisting so noisily and so belligerently that Cole sing "Sweet Lorraine" that he finally did. The response was so overwhelming that from then on Cole concentrated more and more on the singing style that eventually brought him fame.

Words by Mitchell Parish   Music by Cliff Burwell

With a swing

just found joy.___ I'm as hap-py as a ba — by boy___

With an-oth-er brand-new choo-choo toy,___ When I'm with my sweet Lor-

Hard-hearted Hannah
(The Vamp of Savannah)

Like so many others who toiled in Tin Pan Alley during World War I and the early twenties, composer Milton Ager, born and raised in Chicago, and lyricist Jack Yellen, born in Poland and raised in Buffalo, New York, found inspiration in the Deep South, the Dixie or Dixieland that most of the songwriters had never seen. Yellen's earliest efforts were "All Aboard for Dixieland," "Listen to That Dixie Band," and "Are You from Dixie?" while Ager, who had been in Georgia serving a hitch in the army at Fort Greenleaf during World War I, was inspired to write "Everything Is Peaches Down in Georgia" and "Anything Is Nice If It Comes from Dixieland." In 1921 the two began a long, fruitful collaboration that initially drew heavily on their devotion to the South—"Lovin' Sam, the Sheik of Alabam'" in 1922, "Louisville Lou, the Vampin' Lady" in 1923, and, in 1924, their ultimate southern heroine, "Hard-hearted Hannah (The Vamp of Savannah)." Frances Williams, a singing comedienne, introduced the song in a musical called Innocent Eyes.

Words and music by Jack Yellen, Milton Ager, Bob Bigelow, and Charles Bates

Moderate barrelhouse tempo

Vamp till ready

Hard - heart - ed Han - nah, The vamp of Sa - van - nah,
Hard - heart - ed Han - nah, The vamp of Sa - van - nah,

The mean - est gal in town.
The mean - est gal in town.

Leath - er is tough, but
Talk of your cold, re -

Yes Sir, That's My Baby

Words by Gus Kahn   Music by Walter Donaldson

With a light swing

When Eddie Cantor introduced "Yes Sir, That's My Baby," the song fit right in with the current dance craze: It had the jagged, staccato rhythm that was the basis of the leg-flailing Charleston. It had this particular kind of rhythm only because Gus Kahn, visiting Eddie Cantor at his home in Great Neck, New York, in 1925, began playing with a mechanical, wind-up pig that belonged to Cantor's young daughter Mar-

jorie. As he watched the toy jog clumsily across the floor, Kahn, a compulsive songwriter, began improvising lyrics to go with the rhythm of its movement. "Yes, sir, that's my baby," Kahn sang. "No, sir, don't mean maybe." Walter Donaldson, who collaborated with Kahn for almost 20 years, provided a melody for the lyrics, and after Cantor introduced the song, it became one of the big hits of the mid-twenties.

SECOND-HAND ROSE

When a young actor or actress plays the role of a famous star, he or she can easily become buried in the overwhelming aura of the star. However, on rare occasions, a young person rises to an eminence so great that the source of the material is forgotten. Fanny Brice was one of the great stars of the musical theater during World War I and in the twenties. Later, on radio, she had a second career as Baby Snooks. In the Ziegfeld Follies of 1921, at the height of her career, Miss Brice introduced "Second-Hand Rose," which typified her characterization of a girl from New York's Lower East Side. In Funny Girl, the 1964 Broadway musical based on Miss Brice's life, a relatively untried performer, Barbra Streisand, played the title role and became a star herself. Although "Second-Hand Rose" was not part of Funny Girl's score, Miss Streisand recorded the song the following year and restored its popularity after more than four decades.

Words by Grant Clarke   Music by James F. Hanley

Freely

Moderately in 2 (♩ = 1 beat)

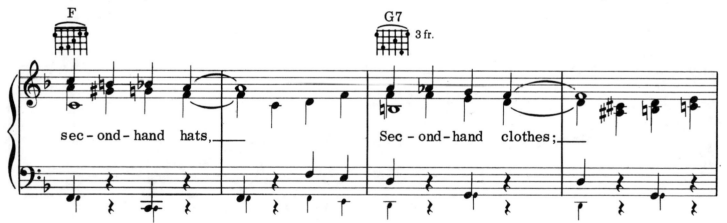

sec-ond-hand hats,___ Sec-ond-hand clothes;___

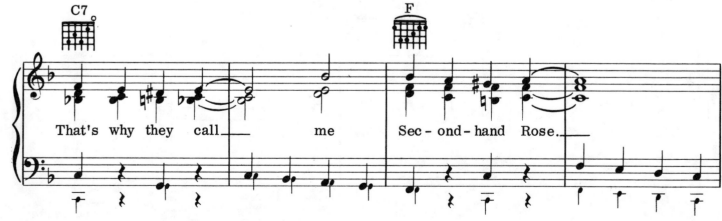

That's why they call___ me Sec-ond-hand Rose.___

Even Jake the plumber, he's the man I adore.__ He had the nerve to tell me he's been married before.__ Ev-'ry-one knows__ That I'm just Sec-ond-hand Rose__ From Sec - ond Av - e - nue.

140

Me and My Shadow

Al Jolson was involved with "Me and My Shadow" but, like "If You Knew Susie," it didn't do much for him. Jolson is listed as one of the composers of the song, but Dave Dreyer and Billy Rose, the other two contributors, actually wrote it for Frank Fay, who sang it in a 1927 revue, Harry Delmar's Revels. Fay at the time had a reputation as a singing comedian in vaudeville. The Revels did not last very long but Fay's career did. It included a starring role in the play Harvey, *in which he created the role of Elwood P. Dowd whose great friend Harvey was a large invisible rabbit. Despite Fay's initial advantage, it was Ted Lewis, the High-Hatted Tragedian of Song, who made "Me and My Shadow" his own. In his routine, Lewis, who admitted that he "couldn't really sing," was followed by a young black singer and dancer who duplicated Lewis' every movement and gesture.*

Words by Billy Rose   Music by Al Jolson and Dave Dreyer

I'll See You in My Dreams

Words by Gus Kahn
Music by Isham Jones

Until the 1950's, when rock began to dominate dance music, each generation of dancers had its own "good-night" song, a song that signaled the end of the evening. Chronologically, "I'll See You in My Dreams" came between "Good Night, Ladies," the favorite during World War I and the early twenties, and "Good Night, Sweetheart," which was popular in the 1930's. "I'll See You in My Dreams" was written by Isham Jones, one of the most popular bandleaders of the 1920's and a prolific and successful songwriter. Jones, the son of an Ohio coal miner, grew up in poverty, and even after he had become moderately wealthy, he clung to his early habits of frugality. In 1924, when his band was playing in Chicago, he regularly passed a music store window that displayed a piano he admired and desired but could never bring himself to buy. Finally, after some months of this indecision, his wife gave him the piano as a present on his 30th birthday. He was so overjoyed that he kept playing it long into the night, composing in those hours three big pop hits: "Spain," "The One I Love Belongs to Somebody Else," and "It Had to Be You."

Slowly

I'll see you in my dreams,_____ Hold you in my dreams._____ Some - one took you out of my arms;

Mean to Me

The "torch song" of the 1920's was a descendant of the "he-done-me-wrong" tear-jerkers of the turn of the century with a slightly more realistic view of male-female relationships. Two of the most successful torch singers of the period were Helen Morgan and Ruth Etting, whose singing styles were at opposite poles. Miss Morgan sang in a high, seemingly fragile voice that was always on the verge of disintegration, while Miss Etting had a cool, slightly nasal voice and a matter-of-fact approach that somehow seemed to underline the emotional intensity of the lyrics. "Mean to Me," written in 1929, was a major hit for both singers. For its songwriters, Fred Ahlert and Roy Turk, it was one of a series of hits that had started the year before with "I'll Get By" and that continued for the next two years with "Walkin' My Baby Back Home," "I Don't Know Why (I Just Do)," and Bing Crosby's theme, "Where the Blue of the Night Meets the Gold of the Day."

Words and music by Roy Turk and Fred E. Ahlert

Bart Howard, who wrote material for Julius Monk's satirical supper-club revues and for such specialized singers as Mabel Mercer, composed this song in 1954. Howard wrote it as "In Other Words," and for years its rise to popularity seemed dubious. To a singer or pianist, the frequent audience request to hear "that song about going to the moon" scarcely suggested the song called "In Other Words," a phrase that was buried in the middle of the lyrics. But in 1962, when the title was changed to the first five words of the lyric, "Fly me to the moon," the song became an "overnight" hit and has been a standard ever since. Another "moon" song had a similar path to success. It flopped as "If You Believed in Me," a phrase that occurred toward the end of the lyric, but was a hit when its title was changed to the opening words and the song became "It's Only a Paper Moon."

Fly Me to the Moon (In Other Words)

Words and music by Bart Howard

oth-er words:____ ____ Hold my hand!____ ____ In

oth-er words:____ ____ Dar - ling, kiss me! 1 2 1 2 3 4

Fill my heart with song, And let me sing for-ev-er-more;

You are all I long for, All I wor - ship and a - dore. In

Dream a Little Dream of Me

"Dream a Little Dream of Me" has had two periods of great popularity, and in each case the singer who brought the song to the fore was, ironically, a woman of ample proportions. Kate Smith made it a hit in 1931, and Cass Elliot—Mama Cass of The Mamas and Papas—had an even bigger hit with it in 1968. The song was composed by two men who specialized in Latin music—Wilbur Schwandt, who was Xavier Cugat's arranger, and Fabian Andre, a conductor and composer who wrote Rhythms of Latin-America. Gus Kahn supplied the words that shifted the tune from its original Latin bias, and Wayne King completed the transformation by introducing it in his soft, slow, dreamy style.

In a lazy 4 (♩ =1 beat)

Stars shin-ing bright a - bove you, Night breez-es seem to whis-per, "I love you." Birds sing-ing in the syc - a-more tree, "Dream a lit-tle dream of me." Say "night - ie-night" and

Sweet dreams till sun-beams kiss me; Just hold me tight, and tell me you'll miss me.
find you, Sweet dreams that leave all wor-ries be - hind you;

Words by Gus Kahn   Music by Wilbur Schwandt and Fabian Andre

I Left My Heart in San Francisco

Tony Bennett and this song rescued each other from obscurity. Bennett's sudden rise to stardom began with his 1953 recording of "Rags to Riches," but his style of pop balladry was soon overshadowed by Elvis Presley and the first wave of rock music. This song, when first heard in 1954, was smothered under an operatic lyric. Then in 1962 Tony was booked into the Fairmont Hotel in San Francisco and found that Douglass Cross had written new lyrics to George Cory's tune, lyrics about San Francisco. Tony put the song in his act and recorded it. The record sold 3 million copies, building a momentum that carried Tony through the second wave of rock, brought on by The Beatles.

Words by Douglass Cross   Music by George Cory

lit-tle ca-ble cars _____ climb half-way to the stars! ___

___ The morn - ing fog _____ may chill the

air; I don't care! My love waits there

in San Fran - cis - co, ___ A - bove the

155

MY PRAYER

Music by Georges Boulanger
Words and musical adaptation
by Jimmy Kennedy

Audiences danced to "My Prayer" in 1939, and in 1956, when dancing was no longer as popular, they listened to the close harmony of The Platters on the same song. The melody was originally written as a short piece for the violin, "Avant de Mourir," by the French composer Georges Boulanger. English songwriter Jimmy Kennedy adapted the music to a song format and wrote lyrics which were introduced in England by Vera Lynn. Sammy Kaye brought the song to the United States for his orchestra to play in 1939, and that's when the dancing began.

Andante cantabile

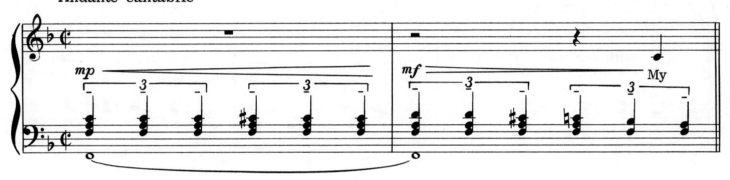

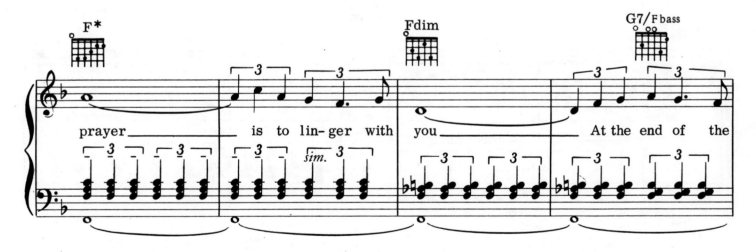

prayer____ is to lin-ger with you____ At the end of the

day____ In a dream that's di-vine.____ My

* Tune lowest string up a ½ step to F.

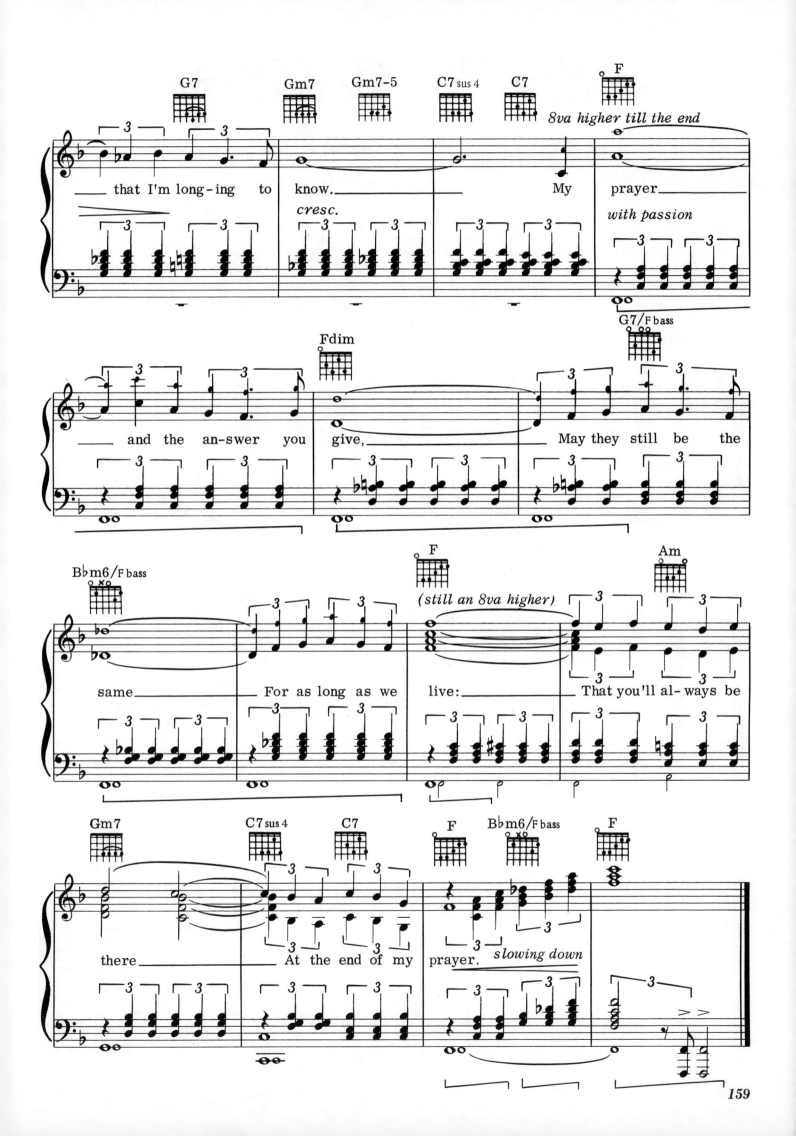

We've Only Just Begun

When Crocker Citizens Bank in San Francisco decided to shed its image as a bluestocking, upper-class institution in 1970, its advertising agency drew up a low-keyed TV commercial intended to attract people in their 20's and 30's. "We wanted them to know that we understood they had a long way to go in life, and we wanted to help them," one executive pointed out. The scene for the commercial was to be a wedding in a white-spired church. As musical background, the agency wanted a ballad to be called "You've Only Just Begun." They asked Burt Bacharach to write the song, but he wasn't interested. Then they approached Jimmy Webb, but he couldn't do it because he was on his way to Europe. However, he recommended a young songwriting team, Paul Williams and Roger Nichols, and they turned out the song in two days. After the commercial was aired, there was a deluge of requests for sheet music from couples who wanted to use the song at their weddings. And finally, with only one word changed —"You've" to "We've"—the TV commercial became a pop hit, thanks to a recording by the brother-sister team The Carpenters.

Words by Paul Williams　　　**Music by Roger Nichols**

Slowly, but with a beat

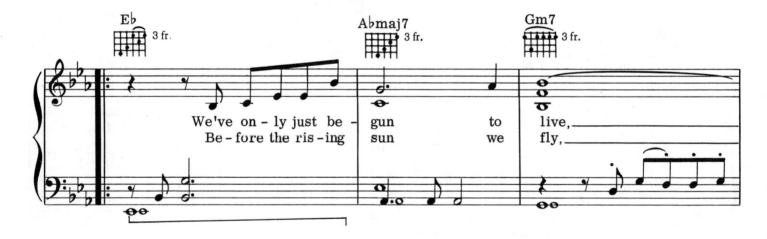

We've on-ly just be-gun to live, _____
Be-fore the ris-ing sun we fly, _____

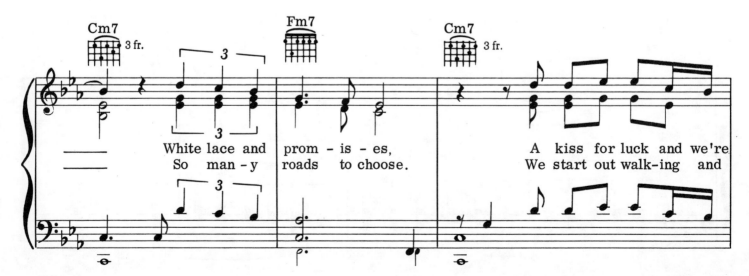

_____ White lace and prom-is-es, A kiss for luck and we're
_____ So man-y roads to choose. We start out walk-ing and

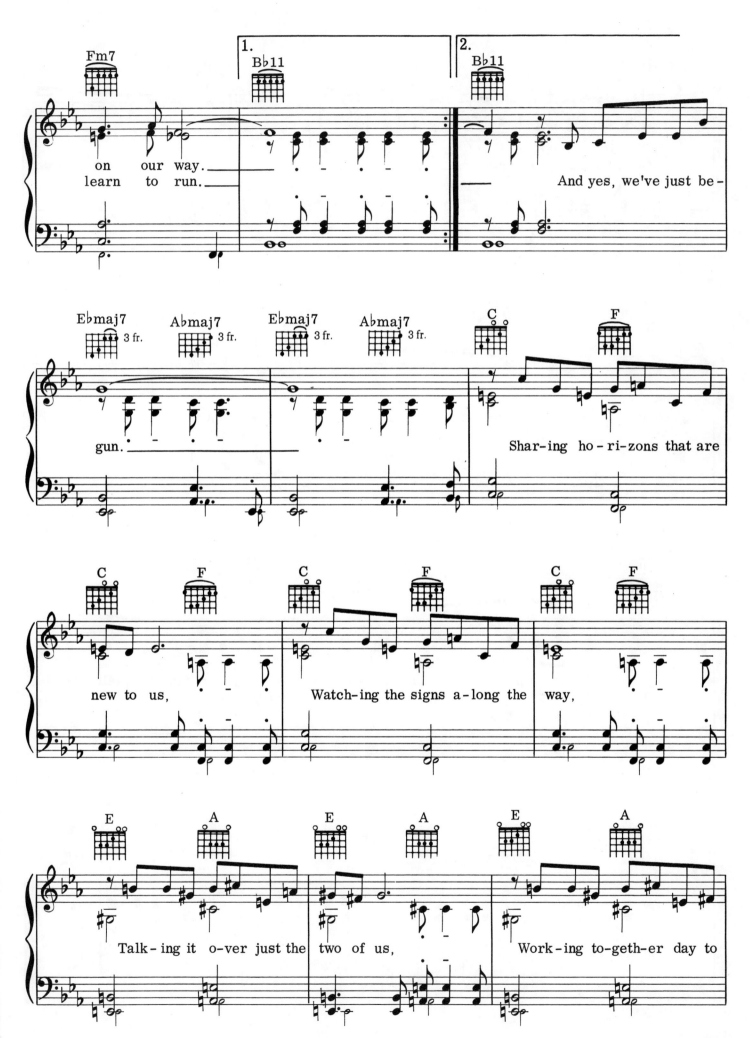

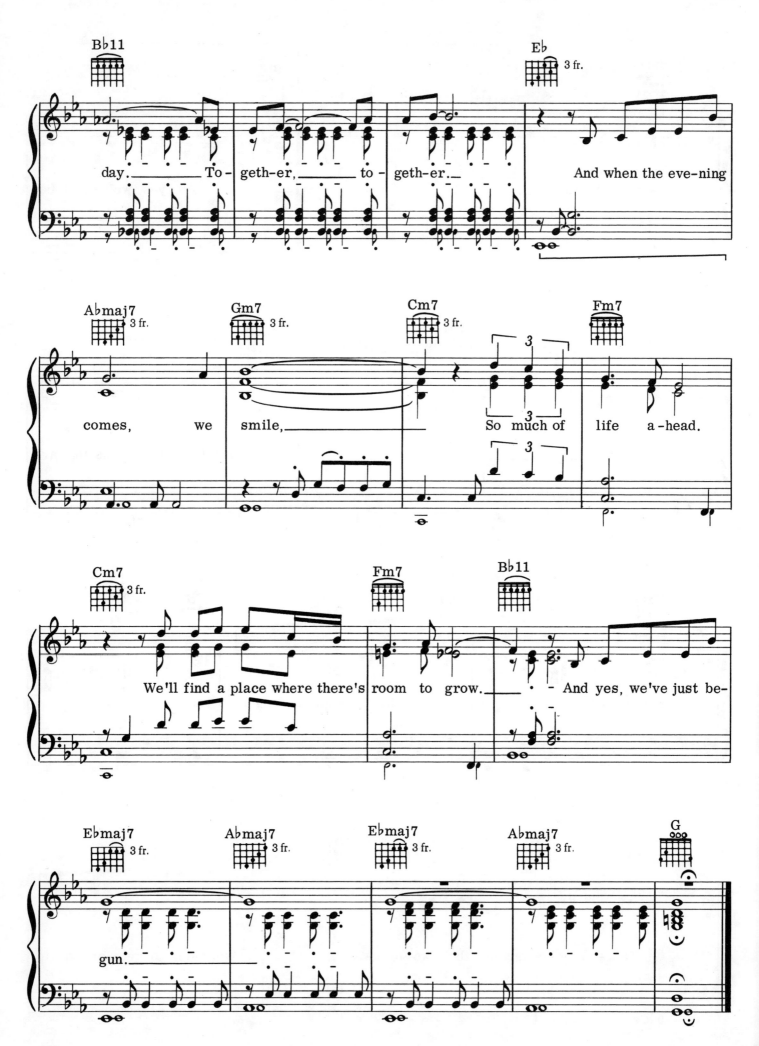

Misty

Words by Johnny Burke
Music by Erroll Garner

Erroll Garner was a self-taught pianist. Because he never learned to read music, the Pittsburgh Musicians Union refused him membership. Unable to play with other musicians in his hometown, he was forced into a career as a soloist. He developed a big, lush style filled with dramatic effects to show off the full resources of the piano. Ideas for his improvisations came from everywhere—"a big color, the sound of water and wind, or the flash of something cool." One idea came to him while he was flying from Chicago to New York on a wet, cloudy day. Since he was unable to write music, he kept humming the melody over and over to keep it in his mind. As soon as the plane landed, he rushed to a piano and put the tune on tape. He called it "Misty" in honor of the weather.

Slowly and somewhat freely throughout

Look at me. I'm as help-less as a kit-ten up a tree, And I feel like I'm cling-ing to a cloud. I can't_ un-der-stand;_ I get mist-y just hold-ing your hand._____ Walk my way, and a

164

When The Beatles' first film, A Hard Day's Night, was released in 1964, the group was still extremely controversial. Their music and style seemed to mesmerize those under 25 and to puzzle or outrage those over 35. The movie gave the over 35's their first opportunity to come to grips with The Beatles—to decide in terms that they understood whether they actually liked the four singers or not. This was partly due to the fact that A Hard Day's Night was reminiscent of a Marx Brothers movie and

And I Love Her

therefore understandable to them in a way that The Beatles' songs had not been. Even one of the songs in the film, John Lennon and Paul McCartney's "And I Love Her," had qualities that the older audience could relate to. Enough like the songs to which they were accustomed, it was easy on their ears without affronting the younger ears that were also listening to it. Thus "And I Love Her" was the predecessor of later Beatles songs—"Yesterday," "Eleanor Rigby," "Michelle"—that gained for them the widest possible audience of any songwriters in the 1960's.

Words and music by John Lennon and Paul McCartney

With a Latin feeling

I give her all my love,— That's all I
She gives me ev-'ry-thing,— And ten-der-

do.— And if you saw my love,—
ly.— The kiss my lov-er brings,—

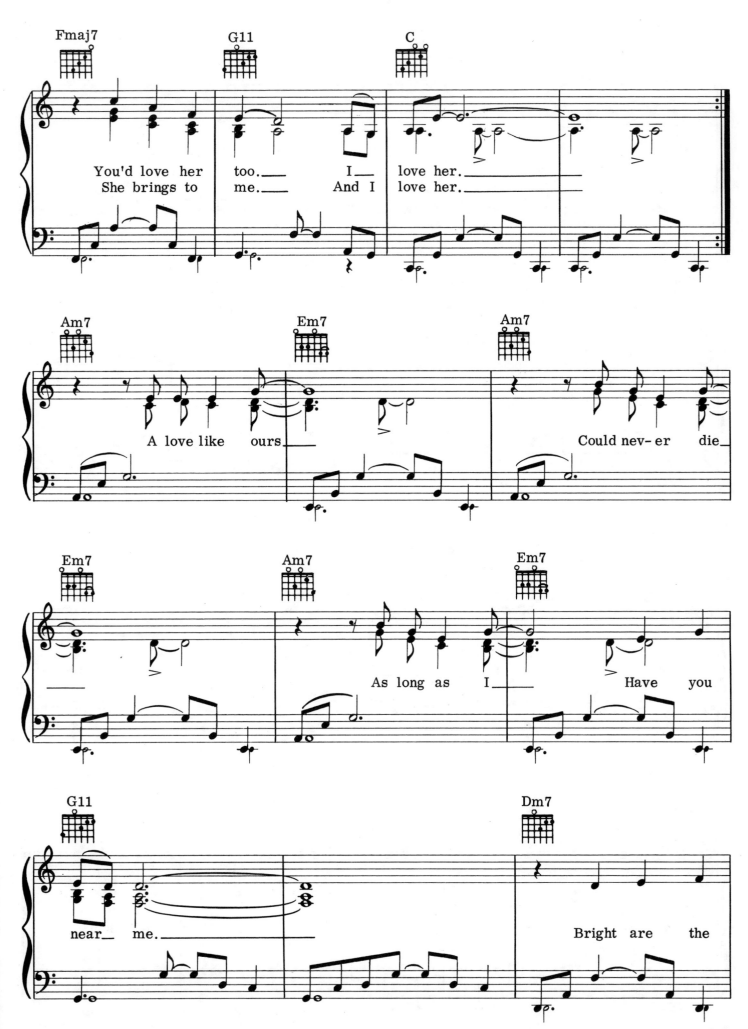

What Now My Love

(Et Maintenant)

Gilbert Bécaud is among those great European chansonniers (Jacques Brel, Charles Trenet, and Charles Aznavour are others) whose careers as songwriters and as singers have been mutually complementary. Bécaud has written more than 700 songs and an opera, L'Opéra d'Aran, that ran for 100 performances in Paris, an achievement more to be expected of a musical comedy than an opera. In 1962 Bécaud wrote and introduced a song called "Et Maintenant." When Jane Morgan, an American singer who had spent several years in Paris, returned to the United States that year, she brought with her "Et Maintenant," which, with English lyrics by Carl Sigman, became "What Now My Love." The song helped to reintroduce Miss Morgan to American audiences, establishing her as a bilingual singer (she sang both French and English versions), and provided Herb Alpert and The Tijuana Brass with one of their most successful instrumental hits.

**Original French words by Pierre Delanoe,
English words by Carl Sigman, Music by Gilbert Bécaud**

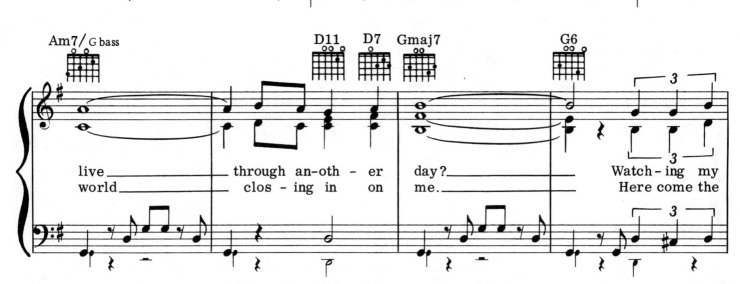

The Fool on the Hill

Words and music by John Lennon and Paul McCartney

By 1967, when John Lennon and Paul McCartney wrote this song, their works had grown from simplistic rock songs to increasingly sophisticated harmonies and melodies and finally to a poetic presence. "Fool on the Hill," written for The Beatles' Magical Mystery Tour album (and film), was a climax to the Indian influences that had been appearing in their works during the previous two years. "Blue Jay Way," "Strawberry Fields Forever," and "I Am the Walrus" were other Indian-inspired songs in Magical Mystery Tour, but "Fool on the Hill" was the most Indian of them all in its philosophical expression. As Allen Keesee pointed out in "Indian Influences on The Beatles," in The Beatles Book, "It alone of all the supposedly Indian songs stresses individuality," pointing up the isolation that is the fate of the genuine Hindu ascetic. The fool on the hill "never shows his feelings and is perfectly still," said Keesee. "He is ignored, nobody likes him, but still he knows that it is the others—this material world and its animalistic population—who are the fools, the trash, the maya."

*Guitarists tune lowest string to D.

172

It's Impossible

(Somos Novios)

The songs of Armando Manzanero of Mexico have affected the careers of several American performers. "It's Impossible," for one, brought Perry Como out of semi-retirement after he made a hit recording of it in 1971. But renewed success hasn't changed Perry's usual casual style; he still sings only when and where he chooses. It's Como's way, and he has proved it's not impossible.

Spanish words and music by Armando Manzanero
English words by Sid Wayne

Freely and rhapsodically

Moderately slow

It's im-pos-si-ble. Tell the sun to leave the sky; It's just im-pos-si-ble.
So-mos no-vios,— Pues los dos sen-ti-mos mu-tuo a-mor pro-fun-do,—

It's im-pos-si-ble. Ask a ba-by not to cry; It's just im-
Y con e-so— ya ga-na-mos Lo más gran-de de es-te

pos-si-ble. Can I hold you— clos-er
mun-do.— Nos a-ma-mos,— nos be-

Yesterday

For several years the artfulness of The Beatles' performances helped to mask the essential puerility of many of their songs. It was not until 1965, as Al Lee has written in The Beatles Book, that "... they began to create songs that deserved literary attention, and not until 1967 did one realize that they had set out to build a body of work that compels attention." This change began to make itself felt in 1965 with "Yesterday" (followed by "Michelle," "Norwegian Wood," and, in 1966, "Eleanor Rigby").

"Yesterday," which was introduced to the public on Ed Sullivan's TV show, was first released as a single record. The idea was to make "Yesterday" as accessible as possible to an older audience that might not expect a song of such delicately folklike flavor from The Beatles. Whether or not such strategy was really necessary, it worked, and "Yesterday" broke through to an audience that had previously been either undecided about or hostile to The Beatles.

**Words and music by John Lennon
and Paul McCartney**

179

section 7: From the Broadway Musicals - Show Time!

I Love Paris

from *Can-Can*

Songwriters may be inspired by a great variety of stimuli. But sometimes the source of a songwriter's inspiration is not quite what it seems to be. Cole Porter's "I Love Paris," for example, was obviously inspired by the city in which he spent much of his life, no? Well, not quite. The immediate motivation for him to write it (for the Broadway musical Can-Can) was a set design by Jo Mielziner showing a panorama of Parisian rooftops. But Porter did *love* Paris, and he was disappointed when no official attention was paid after he openly declared his affection in this song. "He was a little sad and a little resentful that he received no recognition from the French government," his close friend and editor Dr. Albert Sirmay said. "Not to get it hurt him deeply. After all, he wrote one of the greatest propaganda songs for Paris and France, and it was a puzzle that people of secondary and third importance got honors and he was not honored."

Words and music by Cole Porter

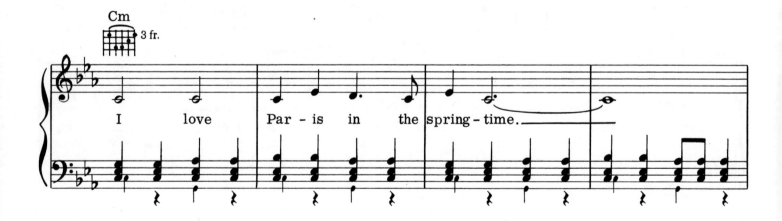

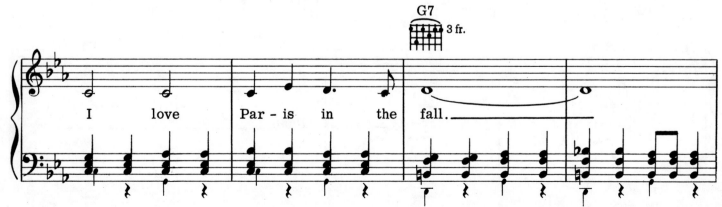

181

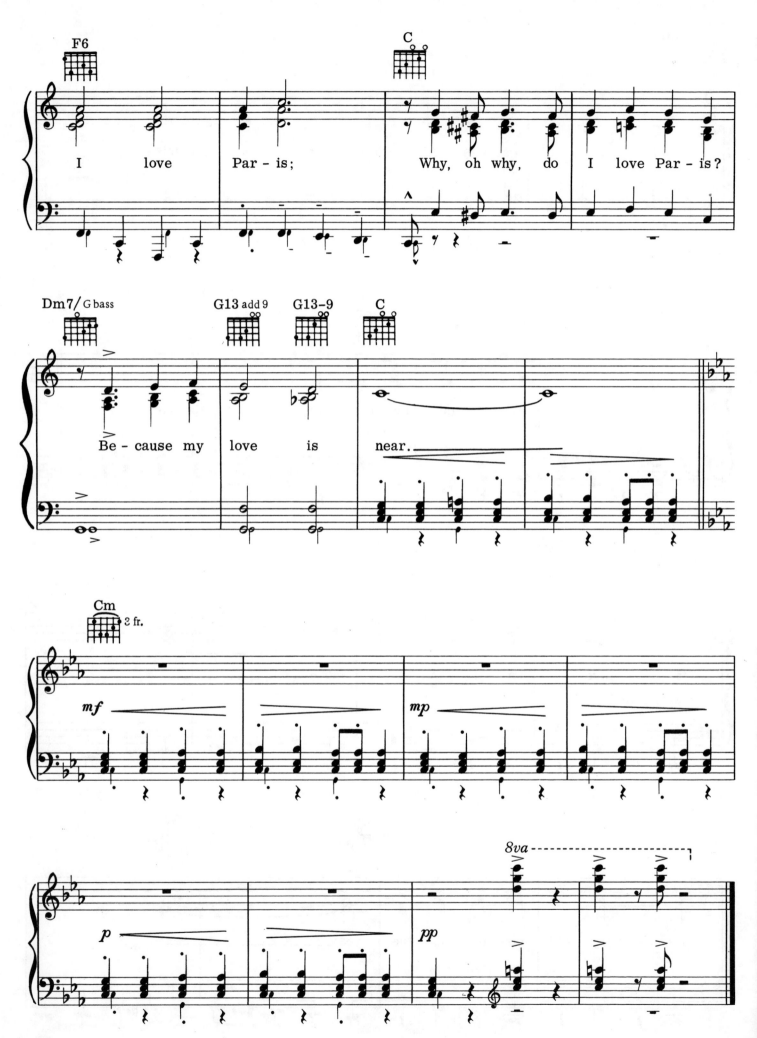

MY FUNNY VALENTINE

from *Babes in Arms*

In 1937 Lorenz Hart used the adjective "funny" to develop "My Funny Valentine," a song that, in much the same way as Ira Gershwin's earlier "Funny Face," catalogued the appealing charms of a face that might easily be dismissed as plain. The song was one of Hart's most touching lyrics, underlined by the warmth of Richard Rodgers' melody. But because of its unusually demanding range it was a difficult song to sing. Sung by Mitzi Green in Babes in Arms, the show for which Rodgers and Hart wrote it, its story might have ended right there. But two years later Judy Garland sang it in the film version of the musical. Judy, who had no trouble dealing with the range of "My Funny Valentine," sang the song so effectively that it became one of the most requested numbers in her repertoire.

Words by Lorenz Hart   Music by Richard Rodgers

Slowly

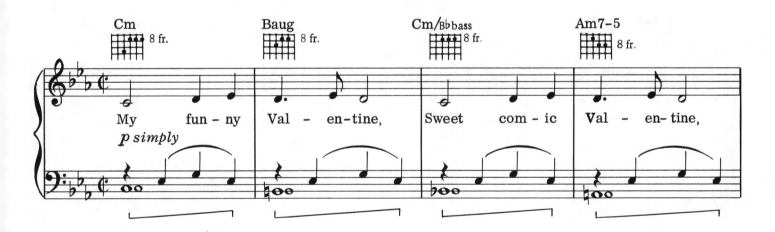

My fun-ny Val-en-tine, Sweet com-ic Val-en-tine,

p simply

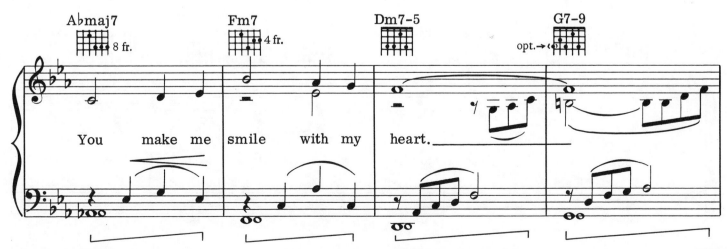

You make me smile with my heart.

I've Got a Crush on You

from *Strike Up the Band*

George and Ira Gershwin originally wrote "I've Got a Crush on You" for Treasure Girl, a 1928 musical in which it was sung as a fairly fast ballad by Clifton Webb and Mary Hay. It was used again in 1930 in Strike Up the Band and this time was a lively romp, sung and then danced by Gordon Smith and Doris Carson at what Ira called "the fastest 2/4 I ever heard." The song was then forgotten until Lee Wiley included it in an album of Gershwin songs in 1939. She was the first to sing it at a slow tempo but with backing from an all-star jazz band, and with Miss Wiley's own astute sense of phrasing, it was a very swinging slow tempo. A few years later Frank Sinatra recorded the tune, taking his tempo cue from Lee Wiley's record, the song became a standard, and the slow tempo became established as the proper one.

Words by Ira Gershwin   **Music by George Gershwin**

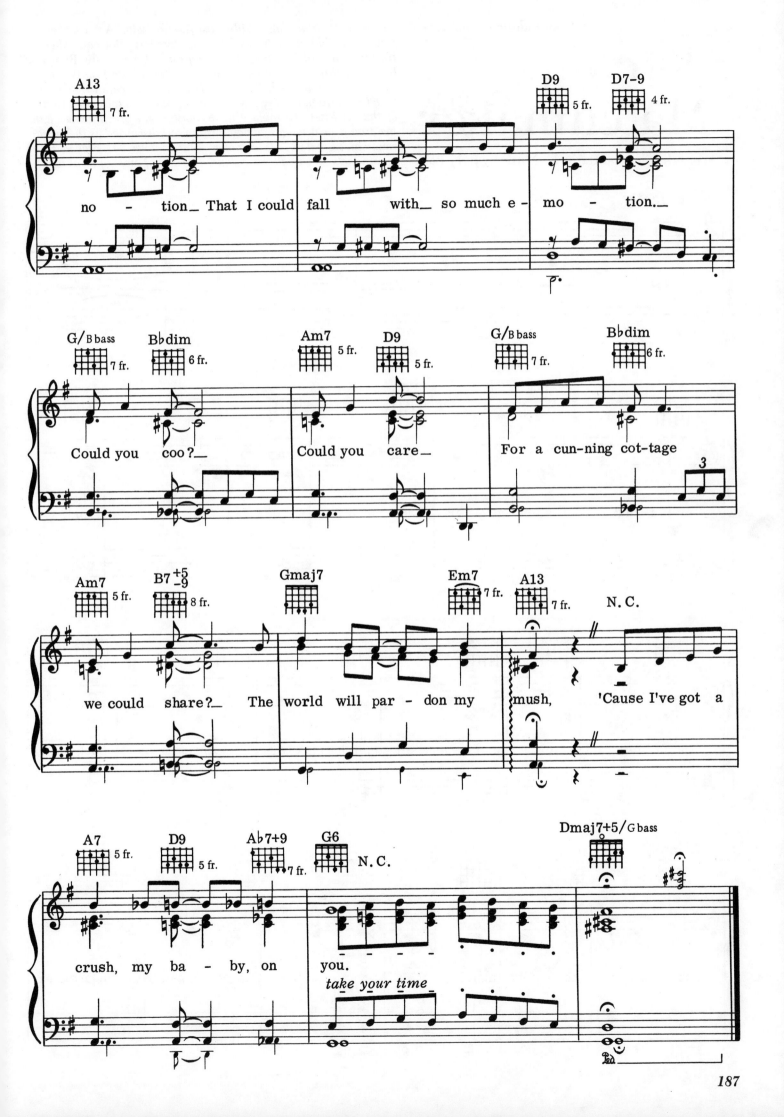

Matchmaker Matchmaker

from *Fiddler on the Roof*

Words by Sheldon Harnick   Music by Jerry Bock

"A wild notion!" exclaimed librettist Joseph Stein. "A musical about a bunch of old Jews in Russia!" Songwriters Jerry Bock and Sheldon Harnick's record-breaking Broadway hit Fiddler on the Roof was based on three of Sholom Aleichem's "Tevye" stories. When the show was in rehearsal, Bock and Harnick discovered that a song they had written for Tevye's three daughters was too rangy for two of the actresses. To replace it, the writers reworked some of the material from a song they had written but discarded as the curtain raiser and created "Matchmaker, Matchmaker." It proved to be within the scope of all three daughters and of most of us as well.

When the curtain goes up on Porgy and Bess, *the first song you hear is this charming lullaby. DuBose Heyward developed the lyric from a passage in his book* Porgy *(on which the opera was based)—"Hush, li'l baby, don' you cry,/Fadder an' mudder born to die." George Gershwin loved his own melody. Director Rouben Mamoulian recalls George and his brother Ira performing the song. "George played with the most beatific smile on his face.... Ira sang —he threw his head back with abandon, his eyes closed, and sang like a nightingale! In the middle of the song, George couldn't bear it any longer and took over the singing from him. To describe George's face while he sang 'Summertime'... Nirvana might be the word!"*

Words by DuBose Heyward   Music by George Gershwin

Summertime

from *Porgy and Bess*

Slowly, with expression (♩ = 1 beat)

Sum-mer-time,____ an' the liv-in' is eas - y;____ Fish are jump-in',____ an' the cot-ton is high.____ Oh, yo'

spread yo' wings,___ an' you'll take___ the sky.___

But till that morn-in'___ There's a noth-in' can

harm you,___ With Dad - dy and Mam - my stand - in'

by.___

slowly

September Song

from *Knickerbocker Holiday*

Words by Maxwell Anderson   Music by Kurt Weill

Kurt Weill's first American musical, Johnny Johnson, was written in 1936, a year after he arrived here from Germany. It was an unsuccessful anti-war satire. His second effort, Knickerbocker Holiday, with Maxwell Anderson as lyricist and librettist, dealt with the tyrannical Peter Stuyvesant, played by 52-year-old Walter Huston. When Weill and Anderson began work on the score, they telegraphed Huston in California asking for his vocal range. "No range," Huston wired back. But he added that he would be appearing on Bing Crosby's radio program that night and would sing a song for them. The writers listened to Huston's rasping, nasal singing and in a few hours created "September Song," the high point of the show and one of the most enduring of all the songs Weill wrote in the United States.

195

Getting To Know You

from *The King and I*

By 1951, when Richard Rodgers and Oscar Hammerstein II wrote The King and I, they had acquired that songwriters' treasure trove, a "trunk" full of discarded songs that could be pulled out to cover emergencies. One of these songs was a melody Rodgers had written for South Pacific that had been replaced by "Younger Than Springtime." During the Boston tryout of The King and I, Gertrude Lawrence, who played the "I," governess Anna Leonowens, felt that the first act could use a song involving herself and the king's children. Hammerstein wrote new lyrics to order, "Getting To Know You." Rodgers had only to reach into his "trunk" and pull out this melody, and the team had created another major song.

Words by Oscar Hammerstein II   Music by Richard Rodgers

Moderately

198

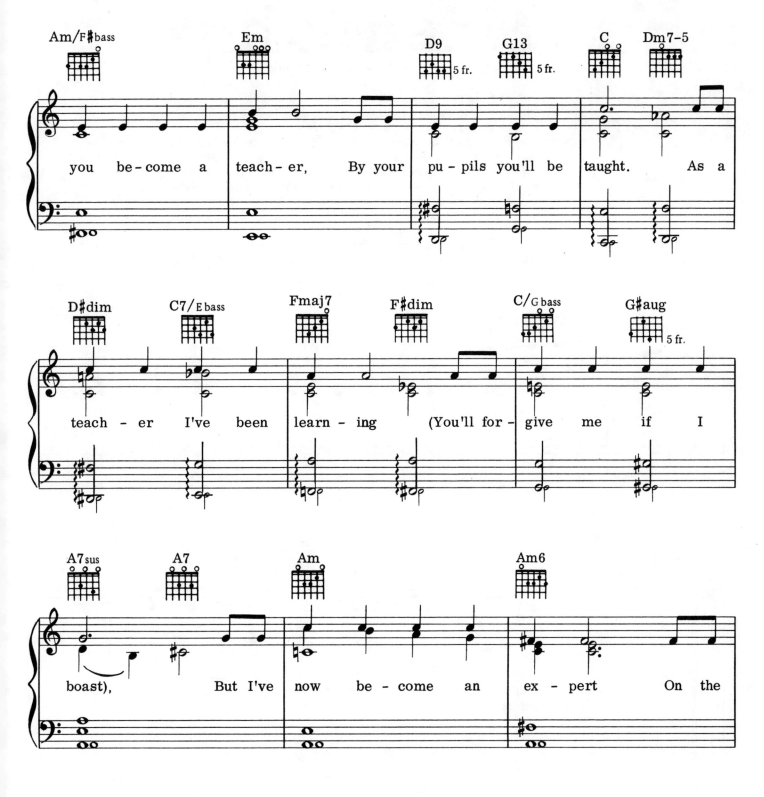

you be-come a teach-er, By your pu-pils you'll be taught.   As a

teach-er I've been learn-ing (You'll for-give me if I

boast),   But I've now be-come an ex-pert   On the

D. S. 𝄋 to Final ending

sub-ject I like most. *(spoken)* Get-ting to know you.

199

Friendship

from *DuBarry Was a Lady*

One of Cole Porter's favorite devices was a lyric that contained long and clever listings. He used the technique in 1928 in "Let's Do It" and in 1934 in "You're the Top." Each was a paragon of wit and worldliness. In 1939 Buddy DeSylva, who was producing DuBarry Was a Lady, asked Porter for a song with "low-level sentimental appeal," so Porter found a long list of variants on the love-hate relationship, which he wove into "Friendship." As sung by Ethel Merman and Bert Lahr, there were constant demands for encores, which Porter occasionally tried to fill by writing new choruses. Sometimes these lyrics were so hot off Porter's typewriter that they had to be sight-read on stage by the two singers who, more often than not, broke up laughing when they tried to sing them.

Words and music by Cole Porter

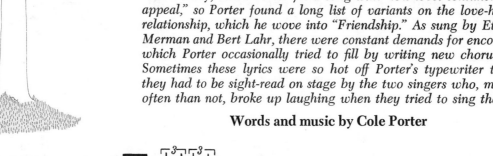

Moderate swing

mp lightly

1. If you're

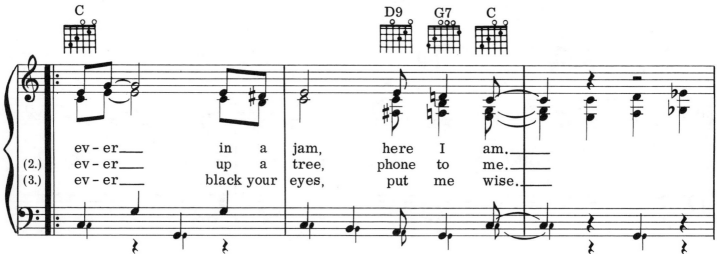

C   D9   G7   C

ev - er ____ in a jam, here I am. ____
(2.) ev - er ____ up a tree, phone to me. ____
(3.) ev - er ____ black your eyes, put me wise. ____

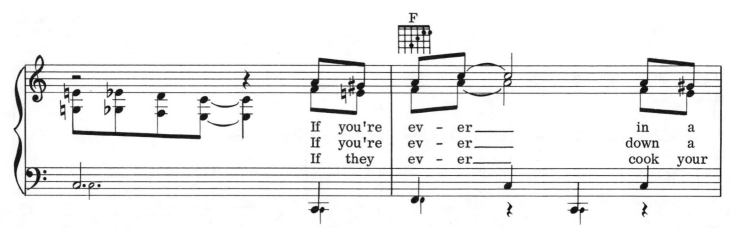

F

If you're ev - er ____ in a
If you're ev - er ____ down a
If they ev - er ____ cook your

You Took Advantage of Me

from *Present Arms*

In 1926 Richard Rodgers and Lorenz Hart had four shows on Broadway and one in London. In 1927 they relaxed—their only Broadway show was A Connecticut Yankee. But in 1928 they were on the treadmill again, turning out three Broadway scores. One show, Present Arms, which included "You Took Advantage of Me," was about the U.S. Marines—an attempt to emulate the success of Vincent Youmans' Hit the Deck, which was about the U.S. Navy. Rodgers' catchy melody and Hart's witty lyrics were sung by Busby Berkeley, who later gained fame as Hollywood's Golden Age choreographer.

Words by Lorenz Hart   Music by Richard Rodgers

Moderately, with a lilt

I'm a sen-ti-men-tal sap, that's all.__ What's the use of try-ing not to fall?__ I have no will;__ you've made your kill,__ 'Cause you took ad-van-tage of me! I'm just like an ap-ple

Bb is the melody, but is played in the left hand only.

On the Street Where You Live

from *My Fair Lady*

In the midst of all the "situation" songs in My Fair Lady, Freddy Eynsford-Hill's straightforward love ballad to Eliza Doolittle stands out in stark relief. The song is one of lyricist Alan Jay Lerner's favorites, although, according to him, composer Frederick Loewe hated it.

When My Fair Lady was on its pre-Broadway tryout tour, audiences tended to agree with Loewe. But when Lerner replaced the original middle section of the song with a verse that was more explanatory, he changed an out-of-town flop into a New York showstopper.

Words by Alan Jay Lerner   **Music by Frederick Loewe**

street where you live._____ And oh,_____ the tow-er-ing feel - ing,_____ Just to know_____ some-how you are near!_____ The o - ver-pow-er-ing feel - ing_____ That an - y sec-ond you may sud-den-ly ap-

208

Here's That Rainy Day

During the forties Johnny Burke and Jimmy Van Heusen were one of Hollywood's most successful songwriting teams. They wrote the songs for many of the Road pictures with Bing Crosby, Bob Hope, and Dorothy Lamour and won an Academy Award for "Swinging on a Star" in Crosby's Oscar-studded 1944 film, Going My Way. But in 1953 they wrote a Broadway show, Carnival in Flanders, that lasted only six performances. "Here's That Rainy Day," from the show, was buried in obscurity until the early sixties. Today it is a cherished standard.

from *Carnival in Flanders*
Words by Johnny Burke   Music by James Van Heusen

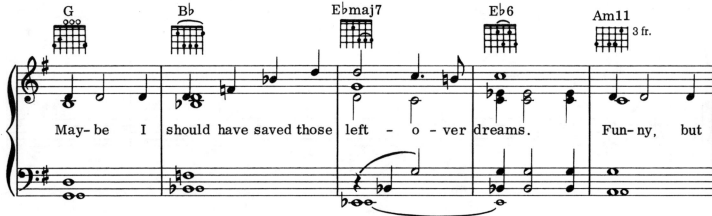

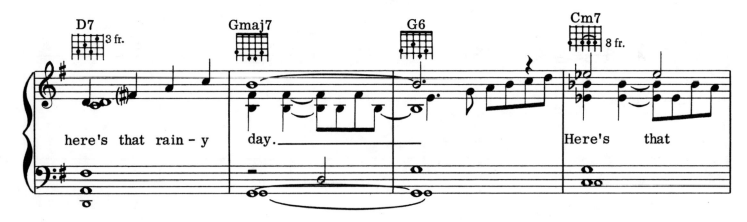

Cabaret, *one of the hits of the 1966 Broadway season, is a searing portrait of the decadence in Germany that led to the rise of Hitler—not the usual subject for a musical. But the focal point of the story was a sleazy Berlin cabaret, so the musical format was really appropriate. The show was based rather loosely on John Van Druten's play* I Am a Camera, *which was taken from Christopher Isherwood's* Berlin Stories. *Ironically, "Cabaret," the most successful song in the show, has been a popular favorite ever since the musical opened, but it gives a totally false impression when it is removed from the context of the show. It has been accepted as a happy, good-time song, played by Dixieland bands and roared out in sing-along sessions. Superficially, it was that kind of song in the show—but it was as hollow and false as everything else in the cabaret. Many who saw* Cabaret *were so carried away by the high spirits of the title song that they missed the point of its performance and the horror underlying the story.*

Cabaret

from *Cabaret*

Words by Fred Ebb   Music by John Kander

Brightly

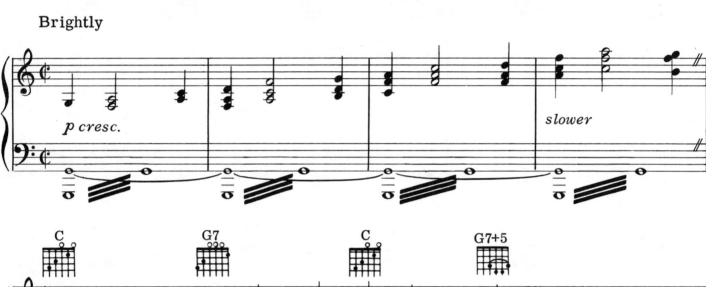

What good   is   sit - ting   a - lone   in   your   room?
Put down   the   knit - ting,   the   book and the   broom;
in tempo

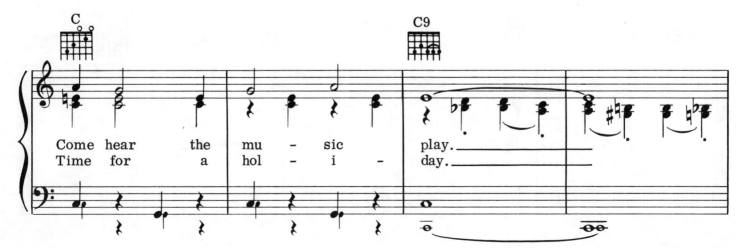

Come hear   the   mu - sic   play.
Time for   a   hol - i -   day.

mit - ting some proph - et of doom _____ To wipe ev - 'ry smile a-

way. _____ Life is a cab - a - ret, old chum,

On - ly a cab - a - ret, old chum; _____ So,

come to the cab - a - ret. _____

ff

214

8va

I Want To Be Happy

from *No, No, Nanette*

Words by Irving Caesar   **Music by Vincent Youmans**

When the musical *No, No, Nanette was* in preparation in 1924, its producer, H. H. Frazee, put on one of the wildest displays of pre-Broadway rearranging on record. He took over as director, had the script rewritten, threw out five songs and had Vincent Youmans and Irving Caesar write four new ones, and replaced the original leads. After the show opened its tryout run in Chicago, Frazee kept it there for a year before finally bringing it to Broadway in September 1925. (He later sent out three touring companies and presented it in London and other cities abroad.) Fortunately, the Broadway opening was not anticlimactic. Part of No, No, Nanette's success stemmed from two of the four songs that Youmans and Caesar had to write hurriedly after Frazee began tearing the show apart. One was "Tea for Two" and the other was "I Want to Be Happy."

Moderately bright

Where Have All the Flowers Gone?

Since the late 1930's Pete Seeger has been a musical Johnny Appleseed, roving throughout the land, dispensing tunes from his vast bag of songs. In "Where Have All the Flowers Gone?," one of his "cause" songs, he deals with the folly and waste of war—not simply the folly of one limited spate of killing but the fateful cycle in which man repeats the same mistakes over and over again. Seeger wrote the song in 1961, having been influenced by the Russian novelist Mikhail Sholokhov's And Quiet Flows the Don. Oddly enough, though, the song made its greatest impact when it was performed by a singer who is as far removed from the rough-hewn Pete Seeger as one can imagine—Marlene Dietrich. When Miss Dietrich recorded the song in Germany—and in German—the combination of language and setting had a shattering effect on those who heard it.

Words and music by Peter Seeger

Inspired by a passage from Mikhail Sholokhov's novel And Quiet Flows the Don *Additional verses by Joe Hickerson*

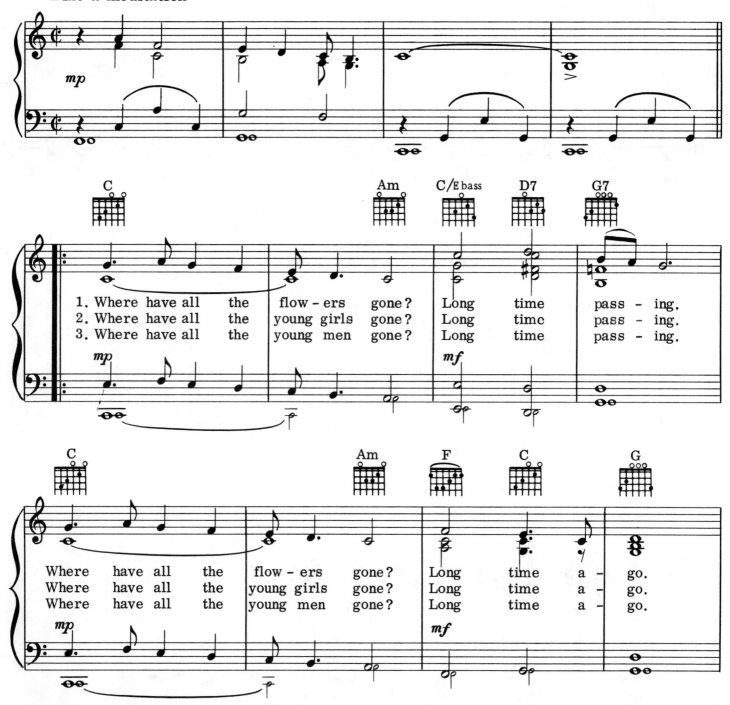

Where have all the flow-ers gone? The girls have picked them ev-'ry one.
Where have all the young girls gone? They've tak-en hus-bands ev-'ry one.
Where have all the young men gone? ___ They're___ all in u-ni-form.

Oh, when will you ev-er learn? Oh, when will you ev-er

learn?___

learn?

4. Where have all the soldiers gone?
Long time passing.
Where have all the soldiers gone?
Long time ago.
Where have all the soldiers gone?
They've gone to graveyards ev'ry one.
Oh, when will they ever learn?
Oh, when will they ever learn?

5. Where have all the graveyards gone?
Long time passing.
Where have all the graveyards gone?
Long time ago.
Where have all the graveyards gone?
They're covered with flowers ev'ry one.
Oh, when will they ever learn?
Oh, when will they ever learn?

6. Where have all the flowers gone?
Long time passing.
Where have all the flowers gone?
Long time ago.
Where have all the flowers gone?
Young girls picked them ev'ry one.
Oh, when will they ever learn?
Oh, when will they ever learn?

Leaving on a Jet Plane

While growing up in Tucson, Arizona, John Denver initially fell under the spell of Elvis Presley. But he soon shifted from rock to folk music, and in 1965 he replaced Chad Mitchell, leader of the Chad Mitchell Trio, when Mitchell decided to shift his focus from singing to acting. For the three years that he was with The Mitchell Trio, as it became known, Denver not only sang with the group but composed songs as well. "Leaving on a Jet Plane" was the last song he wrote before leaving the trio to branch out on his own as a singer. Peter, Paul and Mary made a million-selling recording of it in 1969 that helped to focus the spotlight on Denver's emerging talents.

Words and music by John Denver

ear - ly morn.__ The   tax - i's   wait - in'; he's   blow-in' his horn.__ Al -
think   of you;__   Ev-'ry   song   I   sing__ I'll   sing__ for you.__   When
days to come__   When   I   won't   have__ to   leave__ a - lone,__   A -

read - y   I'm so   lone-some   I could   cry._____   So,
I   come back I'll   bring your wed-ding   ring._____   So
bout   the times__   I   won't have to   say:_____

cresc.   mf

kiss   me__   and   smile for me;__
kiss   me__   and   smile for me;__
Kiss   me__   and   smile for me

Tell me that__ you'll   wait   for me;__

Hold me like__ you'll   nev - er   let me   go._____   'Cause I'm

leav - in'___ on a jet___ plane, Don't know when I'll be back___ a-gain.

Oh, babe, I hate to go.

2. There's so
3. _____ go.

Those Were the Days

Although "Those Were the Days" first caught on in England toward the end of the 1960's, the song had been written in the United States several years earlier by Gene Raskin, an architect who was also a folk singer and guitarist. Drawing on his heritage of Eastern European folk music, Raskin created this timelessly nostalgic glimpse into the past. He first began singing it with his wife in their folk music act, known as Gene and Francesca. Throughout the 1950's and 1960's, the couple worked nightclubs and concerts at night while Raskin pursued a daytime career as an architect and even found time to write a book, Architecturally Speaking, and to produce a documentary film, How to Look at a City.

Words and music by Gene Raskin

Freely

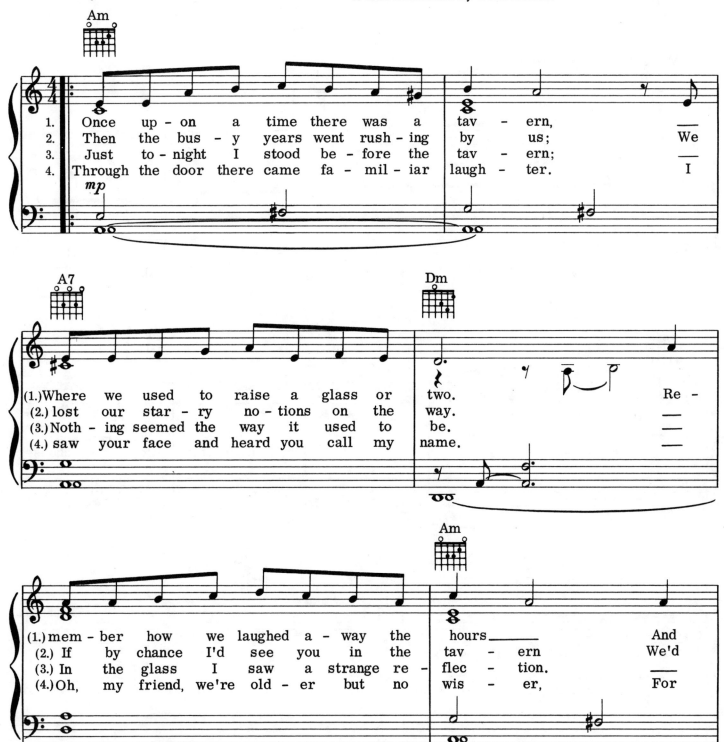

1. Once up-on a time there was a tav-ern, — We
2. Then the bus-y years went rush-ing by us; — We
3. Just to-night I stood be-fore the tav-ern; —
4. Through the door there came fa-mil-iar laugh-ter. — I

(1.) Where we used to raise a glass or two. Re-
(2.) lost our star-ry no-tions on the way. —
(3.) Noth-ing seemed the way it used to be. —
(4.) saw your face and heard you call my name. —

(1.) mem-ber how we laughed a-way the hours_____ And
(2.) If by chance I'd see you in the tav-ern We'd
(3.) In the glass I saw a strange re-flec-tion. —
(4.) Oh, my friend, we're old-er but no wis-er, For

Am/B bass **B7** **E**

(1.)dreamed of all the great things we would do?
(2.)smile at one an - oth - er and we'd say:
(3.)Was that lone - ly fel - low real - ly me?
          (wom - an)
(4.)in our hearts the dreams are still the same.

Those were the

Moderately, in tempo

Am **Dm**

days, my friend,___ We thought they'd nev - er end;___ We'd sing and

mf

G7 **C** **Dm**

dance for - ev - er and a day. We'd live the life we choose;

Am **E**

___ We'd fight and nev - er lose;___ For we were young and sure___ to have our

224

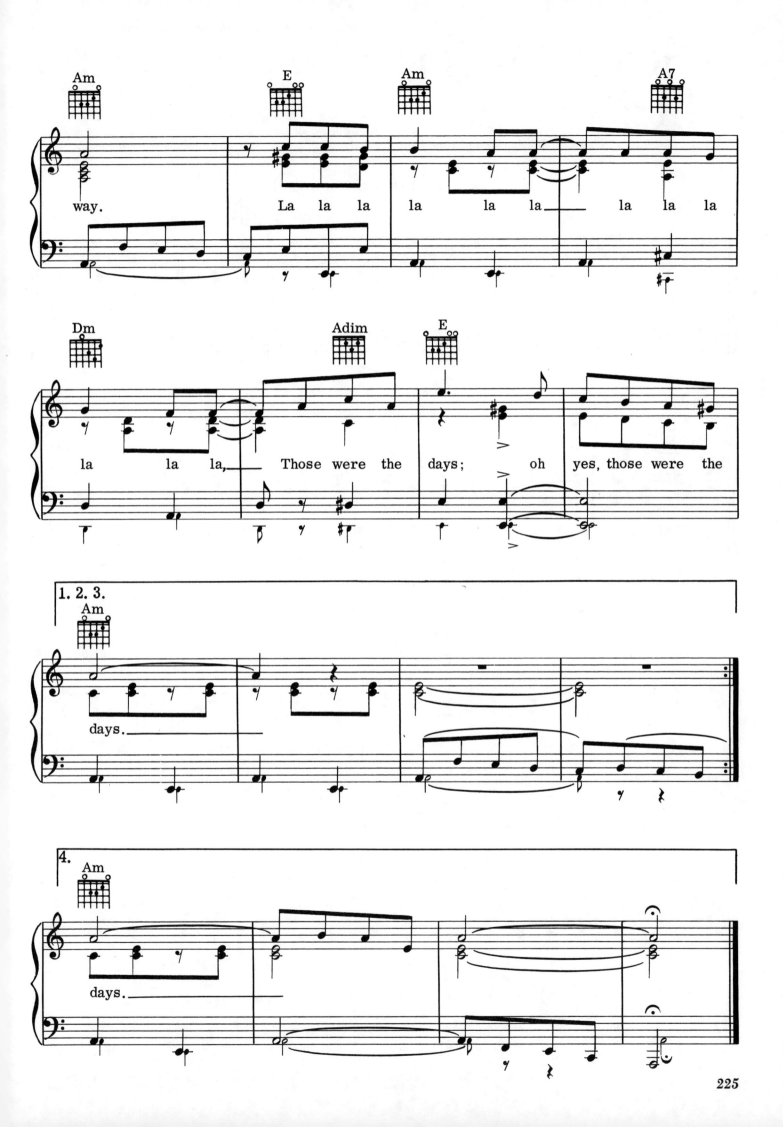

way.   La la la   la   la la   la   la la la

la   la la,   Those were the days;   oh   yes, those were the

1. 2. 3.

days.

4.

days.

Goodnight, Irene

Words and music by Huddie Ledbetter and John Lomax

"Leadbelly" (Huddie Ledbetter) spent most of his early life in Louisiana and Texas, more often than not in prison, twice for murder. His songs sometimes undid the damage his violent temper had wrought—once he was pardoned because of his singing. He first recorded "Goodnight, Irene," a song he had learned from his uncle, in 1933 for the Library of Congress. In 1950 a recording by The Weavers turned into a hit, but Leadbelly, who died that year in New York City at 65, never knew that his song had finally made the Hit Parade.

Me and my wife set-tled down._____ Now
Some-times I live in the town._____
stay - ing out late at ___ night._____ Go

me and my wife ___ are part - ed._____ I'm gon-na
Some-times I have a great no - tion _____ To _____
home to your wife and your fam - 'ly; _____ Sit _____

D. S. al Coda 𝄋

take ___ an - oth - er stroll down - town._____
jump in - to the riv'r and drown._____
down ___ by the fire - side bright._____

Coda

dreams._____

227

So Long It's Been Good To Know Yuh

In his short, painful lifetime (he died at 55 in 1967 after a debilitating illness that lasted 15 years), Woody Guthrie wrote more than 1,000 songs —songs that extolled the land and the people, songs that dealt with social and economic ills. Many of them have gained wide acceptance as folk songs handed down from generation to generation. And like generations of folk musicians, Woody did not hesitate to borrow material wherever he found it. The melody in the verse of "So Long It's Been Good To Know Yuh" is taken from "The Ballad of Billy the Kid," and the chorus is a variant of Huddie (Leadbelly) Ledbetter's "Goodnight, Irene." But Woody turned and twisted both verse and chorus until they had achieved the rakish angle appropriate to his own jaunty lyrics.

Words and music by Woody Guthrie

Chorus

So long, it's been good to know yuh; So long, it's been good to know yuh; So long, it's been good to know yuh. What a long time_ since I've been home,_____ And I've got-ta be drift-in' a-long.

for additional words

2. The

for final ending

long._____

Section 9: Country Classics

You Are My Sunshine

When, at the height of his popularity in 1941, Bing Crosby recorded "You Are My Sunshine" and made it "the taproom and tavern classic of the year," according to Billboard Magazine, the song's success proved that country music could find an audience across the line that then divided it from pop music. Tex Ritter had introduced the song a year earlier in a motion picture called Take Me Back to Oklahoma, but its initial success stemmed from a recording by Gene Autry that helped to make him a star. "You Are My Sunshine" was written by Jimmie Davis, a country and gospel singer who later served two terms as Governor of Louisiana, one term in the mid-1940's and the other in the early 1960's. During his first campaign for governor, Davis spent as much time at his public appearances singing this and other country songs as he did discussing the issues.

Words and music by Jimmie Davis and Charles Mitchell

1. The oth - er night, dear,___ as I lay sleep - ing,___ I dreamed I held you in my
(2.) I'll al - ways love you___ and make you hap - py,___ If you will on - ly say the
(3.) You told me once, dear,___ you real - ly loved me___ And no one else could come be -

230

Cool Water

One of the first singing groups to convey a feeling of the open sky and the endless prairies was the Sons of the Pioneers. The group started in 1934 with three singers whose closest contact with the western prairies was Missouri, home state of Tim Spencer, one of the trio. The other two were Bob Nolan of Canada and Leonard Slye of Ohio. Slye changed his name to Roy Rogers and became a movie star, and Nolan became a very successful songwriter, specializing in songs about range riding, cattle herding, and nights spent around a campfire. His "Tumbling Tumbleweeds" and "Cool Water" are so visually and physically evocative that they create mental pictures even for people who have never watched the tumbleweed roll across the prairies or known the joy of cool water to a parched throat.

Words and music by Bob Nolan

(1.) day I've faced a bar-ren waste with-out the taste of wa-ter.___
(2.) nights are cool and I'm a fool; each star's a pool of wa-ter.___
(3.) shad-ows sway and seem to say, "To-night we pray for wa-ter.___
(4.) feet are sore; he's yearn-ing for just one thing more than wa-ter.___

(1.) Cool wa - ter._____ Old Dan and I with
(2.) Cool wa - ter._____ But with the dawn I'll
(3.) Cool wa - ter." And 'way up there He'll
(4.) Cool wa - ter. Like me, I guess, he'd

233

(1.) throats burnt dry and souls that cry for wa - ter.
(2.) wake and yawn and car - ry on to wa - ter.
(3.) hear our pray'r and show us where there's wa - ter.
(4.) like to rest where there's no quest for wa - ter.

Cool, clear wa - ter.

Chorus

Keep a-mov - in', Dan; don't you lis - ten to him, Dan; He's a

dev - il not a man, and he spreads the burn - ing sand with

Mockin' Bird Hill

Before the mid-1940's country singers had, as a rule, written their own songs. But after World War II, professional song-writers Vaughn Horton, Felice and Boudleaux Bryant, and Cy Coben began to supply such country stars as Eddy Arnold, Hank Snow, and others with many of their hits. Horton's background was completely atypical in that he was neither a Southerner nor a country boy but an Easterner, born in Pennsylvania, who had toured as a sideman in dance bands of the 1930's. His "Mockin' Bird Hill" appealed to both country and pop audiences. Although it became a country hit in 1949, the most successful recording of the song was made by the popular team of guitarists Les Paul and Mary Ford.

Moderately fast country waltz

Words and music by Vaughn Horton

When the sun in the morn-in' peeps o-ver the hill And kiss-es the
(2. Got a) three-cor-nered plow and an a-cre to till And a mule that I
(3. When it's) late in the eve-ning, I climb up the hill And sur-vey all my

ros-es round my win-dow-sill; Then my heart fills with glad-ness when
bought for a ten-dol-lar bill; There's a tum-ble-down shack and a
king-dom while ev-'ry-thing's still; On-ly me and the sky and an

I hear the trill Of the birds in the tree-tops on Mock-in' Bird Hill.
rust-y ol' mill, But it's my Home Sweet Home up on Mock-in' Bird Hill.
ol' whip-poor-will Sing-in' songs in the twi-light on Mock-in' Bird Hill.

One Has My Name, the Other Has My Heart

At the end of the 1940's country stars and pop stars began recording together—Ernest Tubb with the Andrews Sisters, Tennessee Ernie Ford with Kay Starr, and, most notably, Jimmy Wakely with Margaret Whiting. In 1948 "One Has My Name, the Other Has My Heart" was one of several duets ("Slipping Around" was another) that kept the Wakely-Whiting team at the top of the charts for months at a time.

Miss Whiting, daughter of the great songwriter Richard Whiting, had emerged as a singing star a year or two earlier with "Moonlight in Vermont," while Wakely was topping off a career that had included a spell with Gene Autry's Melody Ranch, a stint as leader of his own group (Cliffie Stone, Spade Cooley, and Merle Haggard were among his sidemen), and appearances in numerous if not memorable westerns.

Words and music by Eddie Dean, Dearest Dean, and Hal Blair

Although John Denver established himself as a songwriter in 1967 with Peter, Paul and Mary's hit recording of his song "Leaving on a Jet Plane," he had not yet found his proper métier. As it turned out, jet planes were at an opposite pole from the emphasis that gave Denver his real success, both as a songwriter and as a performer —a quiet, unspoiled, unpolluted return to nature. The key to that success was "Take Me Home, Country Roads," which he wrote with Bill Danoff and Taffy Nivert. It was the song that moved Denver into the kind of pop country territory that Glen

Take Me Home, Country Roads

Campbell had cultivated so successfully. Many followers of country music rejected the idea that Denver, a former architecture student who was raised in different parts of the country and had to cultivate a country twang, should be considered part of their field. But concert audiences and record buyers were not concerned about such distinctions, and, upon the release of "Take Me Home, Country Roads," a million-seller in 1971, they made Denver one of the most consistently successful singing attractions of the 1970's.

Words and music by Bill Danoff, Taffy Nivert, and John Denver

1. G

roads.____

2. G

roads.____

Em D G

I hear her voice; in the morn-in' hours she calls_ me;_ The

C G D Em

ra-di-o re-minds me of my home far a-way And driv-in' down the

F C G D

road I get a feel-in' that I should have been home yes-ter-day,____

San Antonio Rose

Words and music by Bob Wills

One step toward the mixing of country music with popular music that came about in the 1940's actually took place a decade earlier when so-called Western Swing Bands began to appear in the Southwestern states. Bob Wills, a fiddler, had formed the prototype of those bands in 1933. They derived from fiddle groups that played for dancing, with the added impact of saxophones, trumpets, and a full rhythm section of piano, bass, guitar, and drums. It was the presence of the drums and horns that distinguished them from other country music groups. Wills' Texas Playboys and other Western Swing Bands became great regional favorites, although the rest of the country did not become aware of them until Wills' song "San Antonio Rose," one of numerous tunes that he wrote for his band, became a national hit in 1941 via a recording by Bing Crosby. It also appeared that year in a movie of the same name.

Moon in all your splen-dor know on - ly my heart,

Call back my Rose, Rose of San An - tone.

Lips so sweet and ten - der, like pet - als fall-ing a - part,___

Speak once a - gain of my love, my own.

247

Heartaches by the Number

With the Grand Ole Opry as a focal point, country music began to gravitate to Nashville, Tennessee, in the 1930's. In the next two decades, Nashville became an increasingly important music center as country music gained in popularity. But by the end of the 1950's an offshoot of Nashville had developed in southern California—a sort of country music suburb. It was here that Harlan Howard, who was raised in Detroit but nurtured on the radio broadcasts of the Grand Ole Opry, began to succeed as a songwriter. Howard had tried, without success, to break into Nashville while he was a paratrooper stationed at Fort Benning, Georgia. After his release from the service, he landed in Los Angeles, where Johnny Bond and Tex Ritter published his songs. When he wrote this song in 1959, Howard had already gained recognition in the country field with "Pick Me Up on Your Way Down." "Heartaches by the Number" extended that recognition to the popular field when, after Ray Price made a hit country record of the song, Guy Mitchell followed it up with a pop hit recording.

Words and music by Harlan Howard

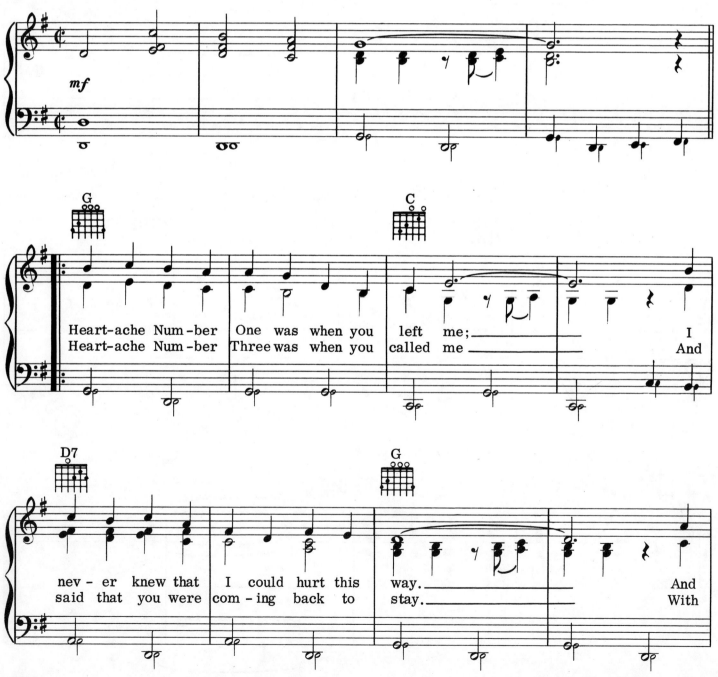

Heart-ache Num-ber One was when you left me;_____ I
Heart-ache Num-ber Three was when you called me _____ And

nev-er knew that I could hurt this way._____ And
said that you were com-ing back to stay._____ With

"Trouble in Mind" was written by Richard M. Jones, a pianist from New Orleans who settled in Chicago. The song was first recorded in 1926 by Chippie Hill, a major black star of the "classic blues" period, accompanied by Jones on piano and Louis Armstrong on cornet. It was one of a handful of blues that survived that era, hitting a

Trouble in Mind

Words and music by Richard M. Jones

new peak of popularity in the 1950's when Ray Charles recorded it. Chippie Hill was not quite as fortunate as the song. She dropped out of sight in the 1930's but staged a comeback after World War II, still lustily singing "Trouble in Mind" and other blues in a full-bodied voice which she said she retained by "gargling that good Gordon gin."

251

mind,   that's   true;   I have   al – most lost my

mind;   Life   ain't worth liv – in',__   feel like I   could

die._____   I'm gon – na   lay   my

head   On some   lone – some rail – road   iron.   Let the

two - nine - teen_ train_ ease my trou - bl'd mind._

Trou - ble in mind, I am blue; My

poor heart_ is beat - ing_ slow, Nev - er had no trou - ble_

in_ my life_ be - fore._ slowing down

trem.

The Entertainer

By Scott Joplin

In the first two decades of this century ragtime was the popular music, and Scott Joplin was the most popular composer of piano rags. He died in a mental hospital in 1917, crushed and impoverished by his failure to get a full performance of his opera Treemonisha. *In the 1920's ragtime passed from fashion and Joplin was all but forgotten, although his first big hit, "Maple Leaf Rag," published in 1899, was still played by honky-tonk pianists. Then, in the 1960's, Max Morath did the first of*

several TV series on the ragtime era, and later Joshua Rifkin, a classical pianist, recorded an album of Joplin works. Then in the 1970's Marvin Hamlisch put together the score for the film The Sting, *using as a running theme Joplin's "The Entertainer," composed in 1902. The score won the Academy Award in 1974, and Joplin again became a musical hero. Ironically,* Treemonisha *was finally produced and acclaimed at almost the same time that* The Sting *resurrected Joplin's fame.*

Adapted and arranged by Dan Fox

Slow two-beat (not fast)

*Small notes optional

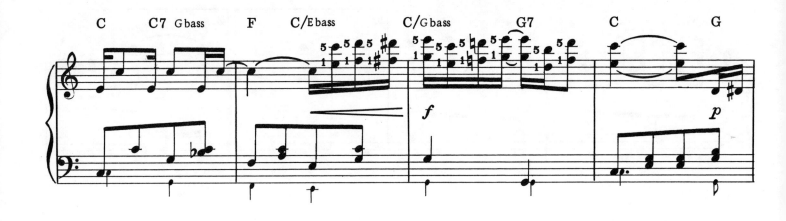

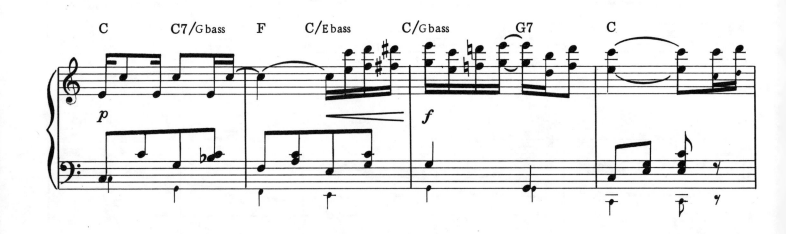

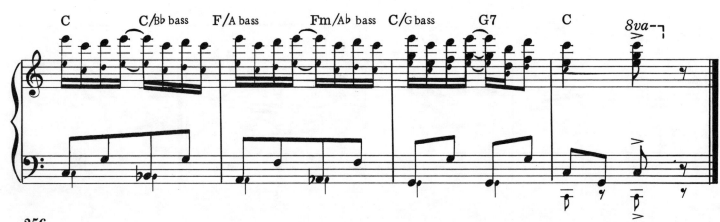

Lover Man

The heartbreak in this song is indelibly associated with Billie Holiday, whose recording, made in 1944, not only established the song but also set the mood for the remainder of her short life. But Miss Holiday was not the first vocalist to perform the song. That singer was Willie Dukes, a female impersonator who, said Roger "Ram" Ramirez, one of the song's composers, "sounded more like Billie than Billie did." Milt Gabler, a recording executive, heard Dukes do the song, liked it, and urged Decca to record it with Miss Holiday. So imitation, besides being the sincerest form of flattery, can also be a source of creative inspiration.

Words and music by Jimmy Davis, Roger "Ram" Ramirez, and Jimmy Sherman

Slow blues tempo

I don't know why, but I'm feel-ing so sad.__ I long to try some-thing I've nev-er had.__ Nev-er had no kiss-in', Oh, what I've been miss-in'. Lov-er man, oh, where can you be? The night is cold, and I'm

so all a-lone;— I'd give my soul just to call you my own.—

Got a moon a-bove me But no one to love me. Lov-er man, oh, where can you

be? I've heard it said that the thrill of ro-mance can

be like a heav-en-ly dream. I go to bed with a

Honky-Tonk Train

Con locomozione

260

Boogie-woogie, a piano variant of the blues built on a rolling repetitive pattern for the left hand, swept the country just before World War II as a direct result of "Honky-Tonk Train." The tune's composer, Meade "Lux" Lewis, first recorded it in 1929. Then Lewis dropped from sight until 1936, when John Hammond, jazz protagonist and talent scout, found him driving a taxi in Chicago. Hammond arranged for two new recordings of "Honky-Tonk Train" and in 1938 teamed Lewis with two other boogie-woogie pianists, Albert Ammons and Pete Johnson, for the history-making "From Spirituals to Swing" concert at Carnegie Hall in New York City. The trio was such a tremendous success there and later at a Greenwich Village nightclub, Café Society, that they launched the fascination with boogie-woogie.

By Meade "Lux" Lewis

section 11: Strictly Instrumental

Clair de Lune

Music by Claude Debussy
Adapted and arranged by Dan Fox

At the end of the 19th century, a movement called impressionism swept through all the arts, although initially it was associated with such French painters as Monet, Manet, and Renoir. Their objective was to create an impression of an object through the play of light on it rather than to reproduce the object itself. At the same time the symbolist poets Verlaine, Mallarmé, and Rimbaud were using the sounds of words to capture an impression. To Claude Debussy the new kind of paintings and poems suggested a new kind of music—a music that would hint rather than state, a music in which a succession of colors would take the place of dynamic development. During the 1890's and early 1900's, Debussy was the prime exponent of impressionism in music. "Clair de Lune," which conveys the dappling effects of moonlight, is the third part of his Suite Bergamasque, composed in the early stages of his development of impressionism. Although Debussy felt that "Clair de Lune" and other works such as "Afternoon of a Faun" negated earlier romanticism in music, these pieces have since been accepted as the height of romanticism.

Performance Note:

All the measures in this piece are to be played equal in length, regardless of whether they are $\frac{3}{4}$ or $\frac{1}{2}$; that is, the time it takes to play a dotted half note in $\frac{3}{4}$ time is exactly the same as the time required for a half note in $\frac{1}{2}$ time.

With great delicacy and expression in a moderately flowing 1 (♩=1 beat)

pp with soft pedal

[*Organ: No pedal till* ✱]

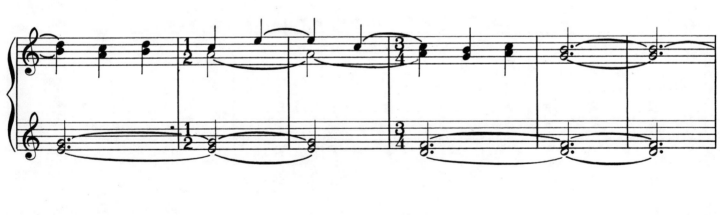

264

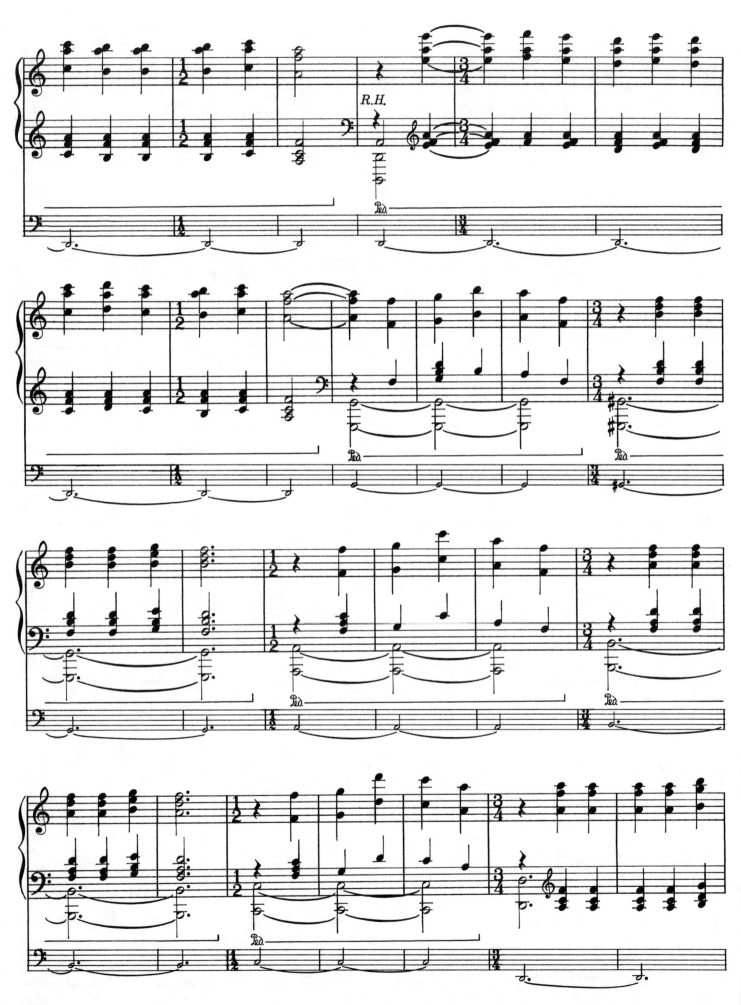

266

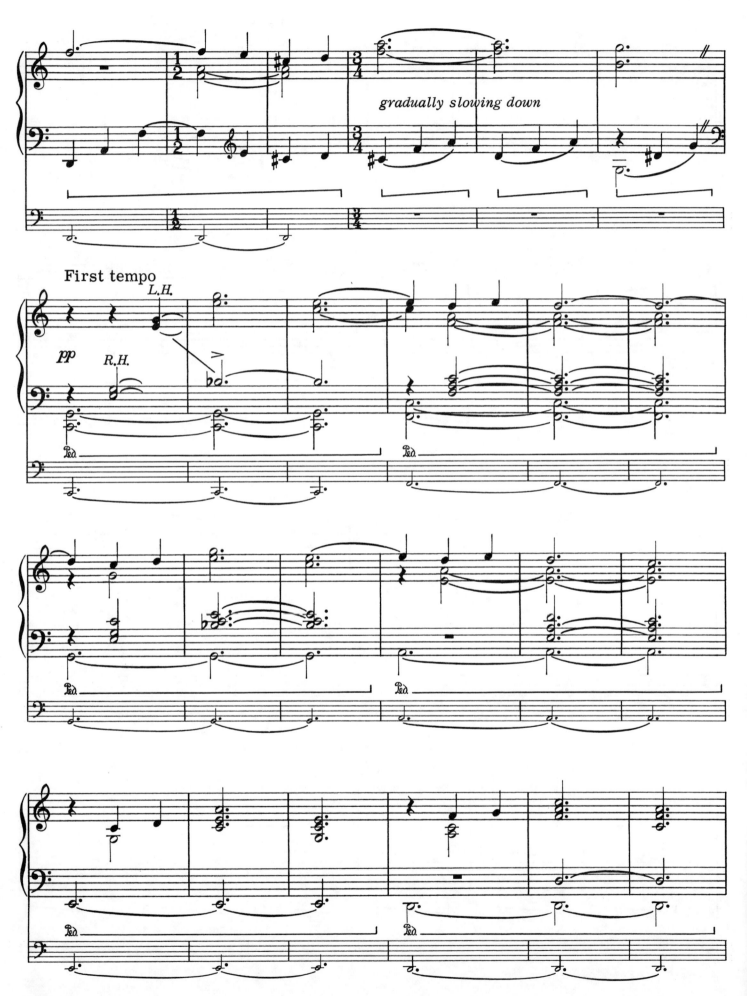

gradually slowing down

First tempo

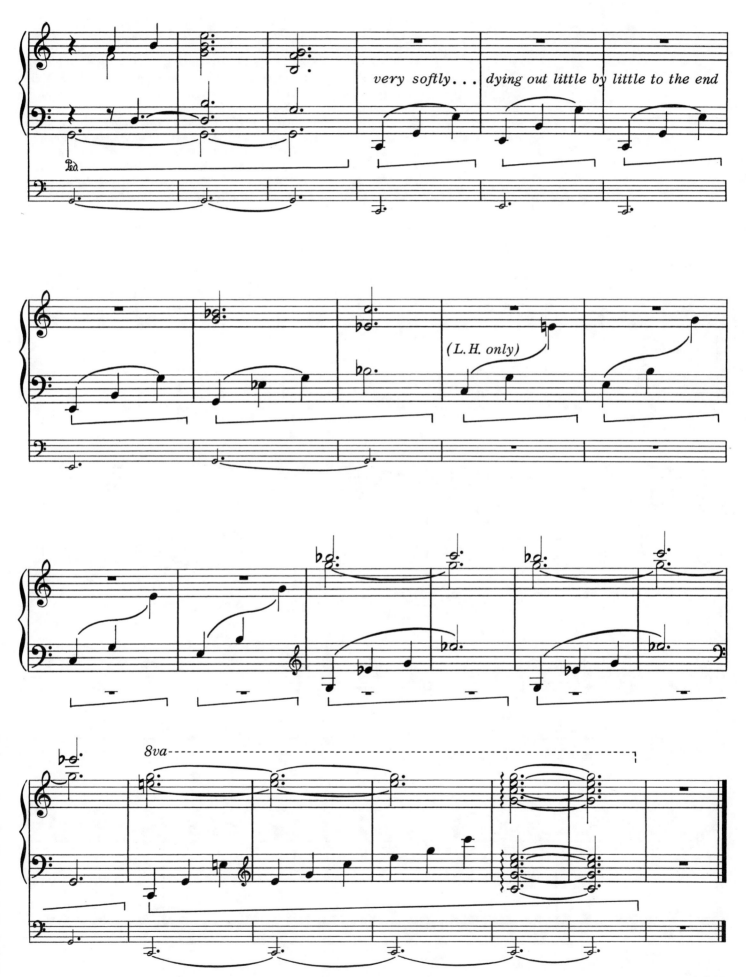

very softly . . . dying out little by little to the end

(L.H. only)

MALAGUEÑA

"Malagueña," based on a Spanish dance from Malaga, was written by Ernesto Lecuona, a Cuban pianist, conductor, and prolific composer. Lecuona himself introduced the composition to the United States when he performed it at the Capitol Theater in New York in 1928, and on the basis of that performance, it might have remained a concert work. But music publisher Herbert Marks, crossing the Atlantic in 1930, heard the ship's pianist playing "Malagueña" as though it were a popular song, stressing the haunting melody. The impact of the melody struck Marks so strongly that as soon as he was able to get in touch with Lecuona, he made arrangements to publish "Malagueña" and then promoted it as though it were a popular song. As a result, it has been recorded in more than 600 versions, has sold several million copies of sheet music, and today is one of the best known Latin American tunes in the world.

By Ernesto Lecuona

Moderately

* *Play 3 times—1st time as is, 2nd time with R. H. an 8va higher, 3rd time with R. H. two 8vas higher, gradually getting faster and louder.*

Slowly and freely

organ pedal tacet till✱

8va lower ----------------- R.H.

L.H. → R.H.

8va-------

f freely

8va--

pp (very gradually getting louder till the fff)

273

* *May be repeated as often as desired, getting faster and louder little by little. You may also double the melody in 8vas.*

** *That is, two 8vas higher than written.*

section 12: For Children of All Ages and Sizes

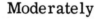
SING!

Like "Green (Bein' Green)," "Sing!" was written for Sesame Street. The objective was to teach children Spanish. For a starter, composer Joe Raposo was looking for a good "sight word"—a simple, short word that a five-year-old child could assimilate. The song actually began as "Canta!," written first in Spanish (Raposo is of Portuguese-Brazilian descent and, in addition to Portuguese, speaks Spanish fluently). The English version, "Sing!," came next. At first it was thought of as just a children's song. But, like "Green," it proved to have broader philosophical implications. Raposo points to the end of the lyric of his song: "Don't worry that it's not good enough for anyone else to hear. Sing! Sing a song!" "It's about living," the composer says, "and about loving and life."

Words and music by Joe Raposo

Moderately

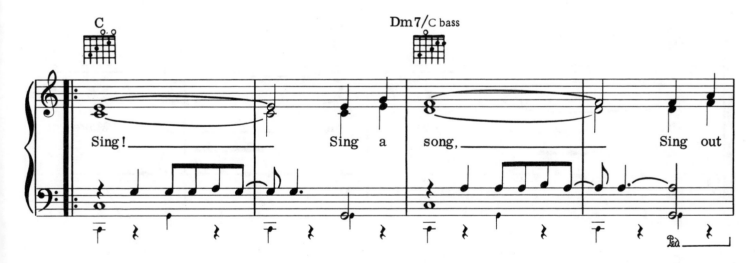

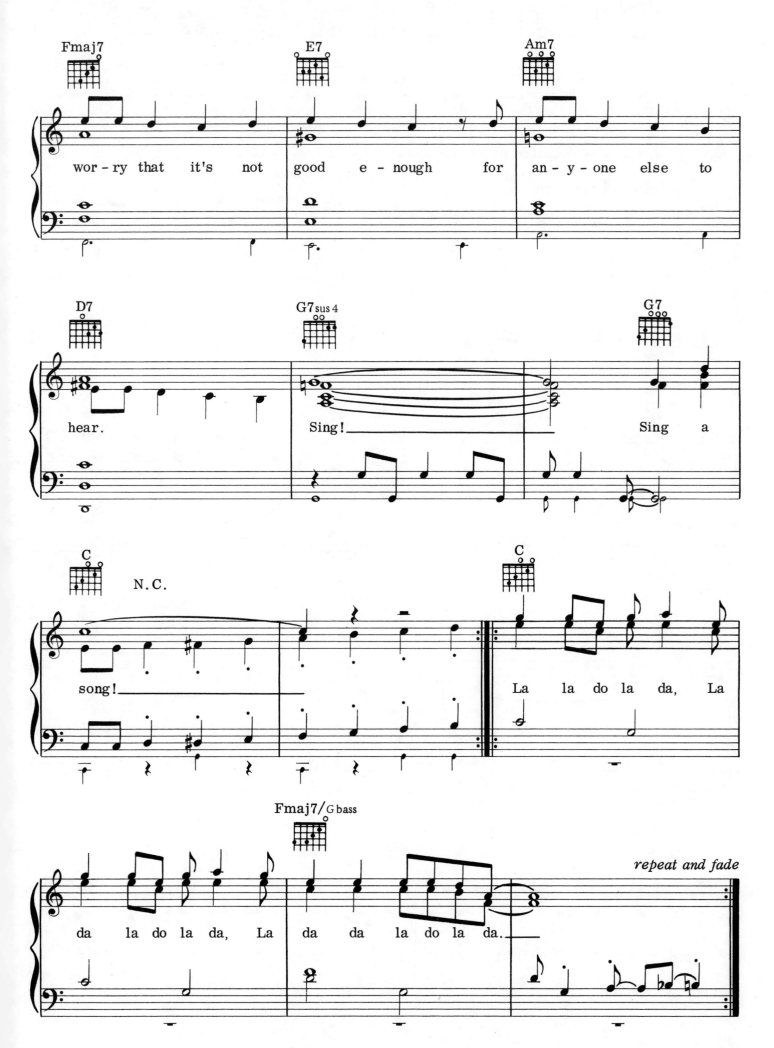

Green (Bein' Green)

It's not easy writing songs for Sesame Street. You get assignments such as "Write a song for Kermit the Frog." Songwriter Joe Raposo realized that there was at least one definite fact about a frog: It's green. From this he developed a lyric that rationalized Kermit's feeling of self-awareness, making the point that some seemingly antisocial beings have sensitive sides. It is a declaration of personal dignity. "A great deal of my own life is in it," says Raposo, "and it became more powerful than I had intended it to be." All sorts of people have seen themselves in Kermit the Frog. Frank Sinatra, whose recording made "Green (Bein' Green)" a popular hit, has said, "It's me." Ray Charles recorded the song. Ministers have used it as the basis for their sermons. And Kermit himself sang "Green" again in The Muppet Movie of 1979.

Words and music by Joe Raposo

278

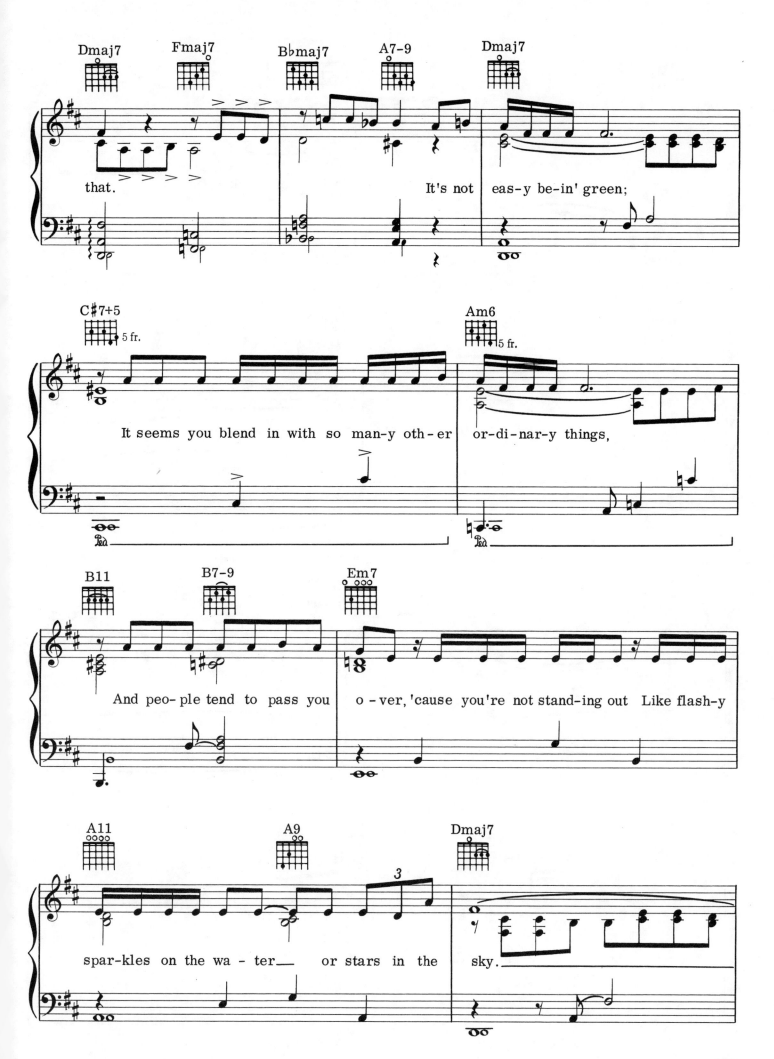

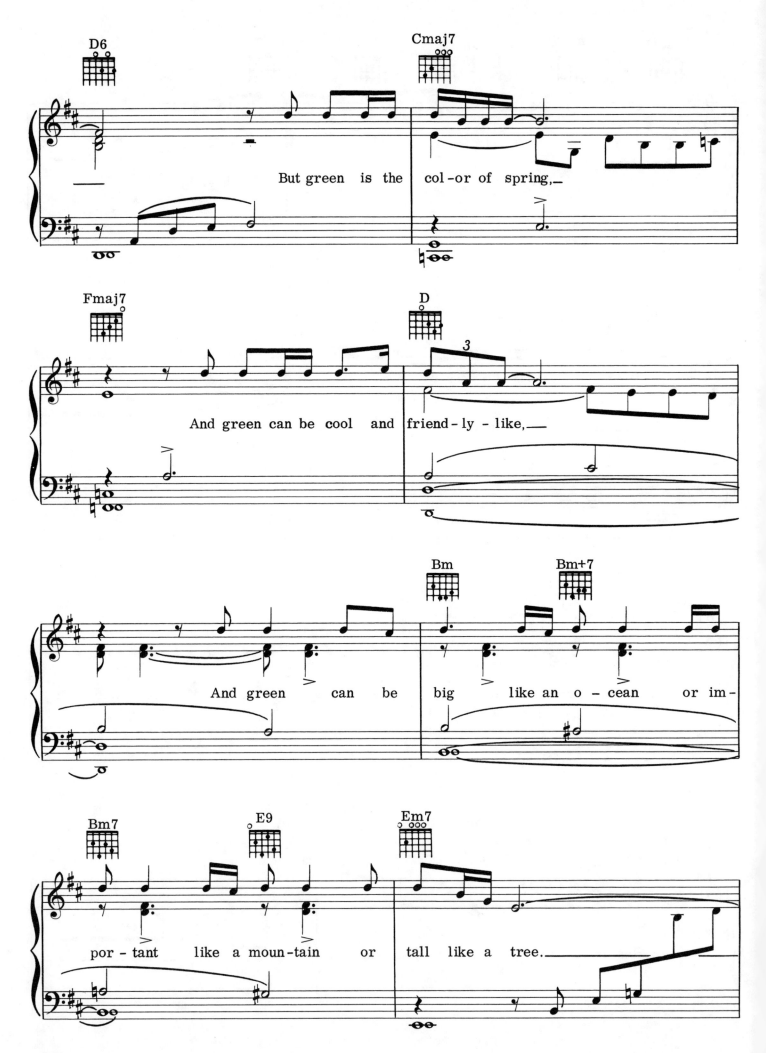

DO-RE-MI

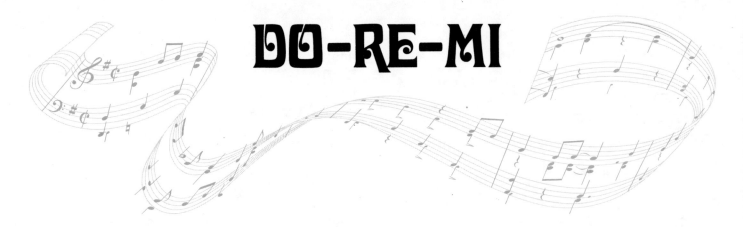

The last musical written by Richard Rodgers and Oscar Hammerstein II was The Sound of Music, suggested by Maria Augusta Trapp's book The Story of the Trapp Family Singers. It focuses on the romance between Maria Rainer, a postulant who becomes a governess in the 1930's, and Georg von Trapp, the father of her charges, an autocratic Austrian Navy captain. They fall in love, she leaves her religious order, they marry, organize a family singing group, and are forced to flee Austria by the Nazis. Maria, a role played on Broadway by Mary Martin and by Julie Andrews in the film version, sang several songs with the seven Von Trapp children, but the most popular was "Do-Re-Mi," built on the ascending steps of the diatonic scale, an elementary music lesson that Maria used to ingratiate herself with the children. The Sound of Music opened in New York on November 16, 1959, starting a run of 1,443 performances.

Words by Oscar Hammerstein II   Music by Richard Rodgers

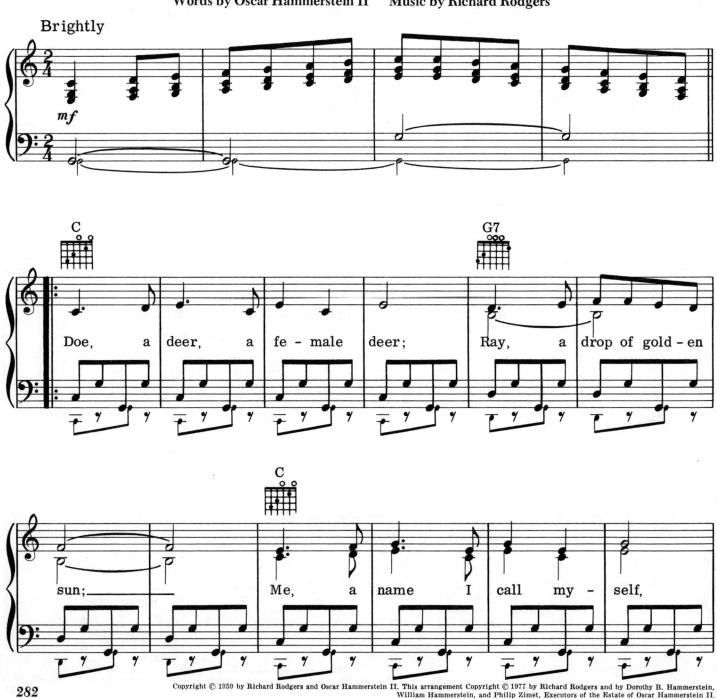

On Top of Spaghetti

Folk singer Tom Glazer developed this parody of "On Top of Old Smokey" after he heard children parodying some of the songs he sang at his children's concerts. Several parodies of "On Top of Old Smokey" particularly appealed to him; so he put them together and added to them. "On Top of Spaghetti" got such an enormous response the first time he sang it at a concert that he re-

corded it in 1963; it promptly went to the Number One spot on the hit charts, surrounded by rock 'n' roll records. Since then the song has been heard in unexpected places. It is now used to help teach remedial reading because it holds the children's attention so successfully. "I never intended anything like that," Glazer admits. "But kids still find it as hilarious as ever."

Words and music by Tom Glazer

Moderately in 1 (♩. = 1 beat)

On top of spa-

ghet - ti,_____ all cov-ered with cheese,_____
(2.) gar - den_____ and un - der a bush,_____
(3.) cov - ered_____ with beau - ti - ful moss;_____

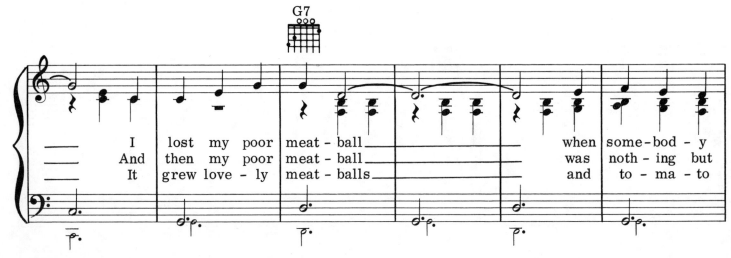

____ I lost my poor meat - ball_____ when some-bod - y
____ And then my poor meat - ball_____ was noth - ing but
____ It grew love - ly meat - balls_____ and to - ma - to

Rudolph the Red-Nosed Reindeer

Lightly

Words and music by Johnny Marks

Ru-dolph, the red-nosed rein-deer, Had a ver-y shin - y nose,

And if you ev - er saw it, You would e-ven say it glows.

Rudolph's red nose has not only guided Santa's sleigh every Christmas since 1949, it has also proved a gold mine for Johnny Marks, who wrote the beloved song. Along with Irving Berlin's "White Christmas," it is the most consistent income-producing song in the world. Actually, Rudolph was dreamed up in 1939 by Robert L. May, an advertising copywriter for Montgomery Ward, who made him the hero of a story pamphlet to be given away in the stores at Christmastime. The pamphlet was a popular success for 10 years before Marks wrote the song. Then he could not convince anyone to publish or record it. So he formed his own publishing company, St. Nicholas Music, and went after a most unlikely singer—western star Gene Autry. At first Autry was not interested, but his wife fell in love with Rudolph. Gene's recording of the song was released on September 19, 1949, and by Christmas it had sold over 1 million copies. Today Marks, as both writer and publisher, collects all royalties from record and sheet-music sales of the song and from all its radio and TV performances too. And he may continue to do so well into the next century, when his copyright runs out.